Ambitious Dreams
The Values Program
at Le Moyne College

Donald J. Kirby
William R. Barnett
Thomas V. Curley
Mary Ann Donnelly
William Howard Holmes
William Miller
Bruce M. Shefrin
Krystine Batcho Yaworsky

Foreword by Parker J. Palmer

Sheed & Ward

Sheed & Ward™ is a service of National Catholic Reporter Publishing
Company, Inc.

Library of Congress Cataloguing in Process

ISBN: 1-55612-412-0

Published by: Sheed & Ward
115 E. Armour Blvd. P.O. Box 419492
Kansas City, MO 64141-6492

To order, call: (800) 333-7373

Contents

Foreword

"Values" is a word that usually gives me vertigo. Though the word points to the most crucial questions of our lives (What do I care about? What will I give my life to?), it is a vague and airy term, often used in rhetoric so pious and abstract that it floats miles above the messiness in which human life is lived. This atmospheric tendency is especially pronounced in academic circles where language too often substitutes for living, and where abstract "values" talk is too often an evasion of real-life questions that might contaminate the academy's ideal of an antiseptic classroom.

But the faculty, students, and administration of Le Moyne College have created a Values Program that refuses to hide behind abstractions—as you will soon find out by reading this down-to-earth report. Instead, they have had the courage to explore value questions by looking at the gaps and the convergences between what we say and how we live. They have done this not only with the students (who are easy targets) but with the faculty, with the administrators, and with the life of the college itself.

The Le Moyne College Values Program has asked faculty to consider critical world issues like war and poverty in terms of their own disciplines. It has asked them to explore pedagogies designed not for the delivery of inert information but for the exploration of basic commitments. And the program has challenged faculty to use these learnings to transform their classrooms.

Of course, the goal of all this work is transformation in the lives of students—a transformation that will send them into the world not only as men and women of knowledge but as agents of justice, peace, and compassion. It is a transformation devoutly to be desired among the circles of the well-educated. Too often, our education sets us apart from the world and its struggles; too often, we are educated away from human relatedness rather than toward it. The ancient notion that "knowledge is power" has become the hubris of the modern age. We teach the arrogance of mastery rather than the humility of compassion and community.

The aim of the Le Moyne College Values Program is nothing less than to renew our capacity for community, our capacity to acknowledge our relatedness to other beings and to make choices that honor those relationships. The grounding of the program is nothing less than—dare I use the word?—truth. This ancient and honorable concept is in disrepute in the modern world, a world so often battered by this and that fanatic version of truth that it has taken refuge in cheap relativism: "One truth for you, another truth for me, and never mind the difference." But at Le Moyne College, there is a willingness to reclaim the simple fact that if we do not learn to hang together, we will hang separately.

Some may fear that at a college like Le Moyne, rooted as it is in a religious tradition, a Values Program grounded in a respect for truth will turn out to be indoctrination masquerading as education. But such fears will find no sustenance here. On the contrary, the Le Moyne Values Program is grounded in a view of truth that is as hospitable to authentic diversity as it is hostile to cheap relativism.

"Truth is an eternal conversation about things that matter conducted with passion and discipline." That personal image, which has guided my teaching in recent years, may reflect the spirit behind the kind of teaching and learning described in this report. The Le Moyne College Values Program strives not to teach students the conclusions of a valuing process, but the passion and discipline of the process itself. The program tries to bring students into truth by teaching them how to participate in humankind's endless, demanding, and exhilarating conversation over what commands our commitment and care.

As if all this were not enough, there is one more reason why this book is well worth reading. There are many people in the academy who say they would like to do something like the Le Moyne Values Program—but the obstacles between them and their dream, they say, are too numerous and too imposing. They cite student apathy, faculty resistance, administrative indifference. But here is a book about real people at a real college facing real issues and still furthering their "ambitious dream." Such a book should help deflate the excuses that too many academics use to cover their fear of taking on the crucial issues of value formation.

Fear, of course, is the main reason for the academy's neglect of value issues—fear of getting in over our heads, of loosing the Furies, of facing turmoil and conflict, of losing control. The long and elaborate argument for value-free rationality is, I am convinced, nothing more than a complicated evasion of elemental human fear. But at Le Moyne College there are people willing to walk into their fears for the sake of a more humane vision. The result is the same one we find whenever persons or institutions refuse to let fear dominate their lives—an increase of vitality, humanity, community, and sense of purpose on the Le Moyne College campus.

We owe a debt to these adventurers, not only for the skillful program they have created but for the care and honesty with which they have told their story here. May such people multiply in the academy, and may their work continue to flourish.

Parker J. Palmer

Preface

A Brief History of the Values Program

This book outlines the evolution of the Values Program at Le Moyne College since the fall of 1985, when it was founded by seven members of the college community. Rev. Donald J. Kirby, S.J., associate professor of Religious Studies, organized the group, whose other members were William R. Barnett, associate professor of Religious Studies; Mary Ann Donnelly, associate professor of Business Administration; Edward J. Gorman, director of admissions; John W. Langdon, professor of History; Bruce M. Shefrin, associate professor of Political Science; and Krystine B. Yaworsky, associate professor of Psychology. From the outset, the members of the group shared a vexing impression that modern college graduates were being poorly prepared to function in a pluralistic society which demands that they make significant decisions without providing them with a commonly held set of values on which to base those decisions. Intent not upon constructing such a set, but upon finding ways to alert college students to the values-laden components and consequences of their actions, the group proceeded tentatively and cautiously throughout its first year.

Habits of the Heart, a 1985 best-seller by Robert N. Bellah and others, provided the group with a set of perspectives critical of the self-centered individualism that characterizes many aspects of modern American life. Weekly and bi-weekly discussions of this and other readings enabled the members to appraise their own and other's reactions and to begin to formulate possible courses of action. By the spring of 1986, we were constructing "building blocks" for the foundation of what would later be known as the Values Program. That summer we employed the consulting services of two experienced grantswriters (John Blasi and Barbara Davis), and with their help prepared our first applications for funding for a project that would consist of a "summer institute" for faculty on a values-laden theme, followed by an "academic forum" that would involve the entire college community during the subsequent academic year.

Success crowned some, but not all, of the group's efforts. Our applications to the Consortium for the Advancement of Private Higher Education (CAPHE) and the Raskob Foundation were successful, some others were not. So by the summer of 1987 we were assured of the necessary funding to launch the 1988 Summer Institute on the theme of economic justice. The CAPHE grant also covered the 1989 Institute on peace and war, so that the group was able to devote a substantial portion of the 1987-88 academic year to planning rather than fund-raising. By this time, the membership had been broadened beyond the original seven members to include additional professors and administrators. Interested students began meeting with the group in 1989 and, as this is being written, the 1990 Summer Institute on families and public policies is underway.

What follows is the detailed story of the Values Program at Le Moyne College. Told from a variety of perspectives, it offers insights into the joys and sorrows of participation in a faculty-initiated program at a small college. The project's impact is multidimensional and difficult to assess with precision, but its achievements, however extensive they may be, could not have come to pass without the faith, foresight, and dedication of many individuals and organizations.

In particular, we wish to acknowledge three faculty who came to the program at the time when we were beginning to wonder how to sustain such a program, insure that it continues to thrive and prosper despite inevitable changes in personnel, faculty leadership, etc. The addition of Thomas V. Curley proved especially critical, not only because of his balance and collaborative skills, but also because he was able to make the Values Program one of his priorities over the next four years. He ably directed the Values Program in 1989-1990 during Donald Kirby's sabbatical. William Miller also deserves special recognition. In chapter 6 he tells the story of why he became involved in the values program in 1988. What the chapter does not tell is the impact he has made on the consequent development of the program. His insight, gentle patience, and leadership in the role of associate director of the Values Program, made a very complex undertaking more manageable. The critical leadership, vision, and administrative skills of both these faculty members are woven in the very fabric of the values program. Also, if William Holmes had not joined forces with Krystine Yaworsky, the critical evaluation and assessment would have been very burdensome indeed. Because they work in a medium-size liberal arts college with neither graduate assistants nor large funding sources, their chapter reflects only a tiny portion of their most creative work.

We wish also to express our deep appreciation to those who have underwritten our efforts: the Consortium for the Advancement of Private Higher Education; the Raskob Foundation for Catholic Activities; a foundation which wishes to remain anonymous and which provided us with a generous donation; the Amos Foundation; the Dewar Fund of Saint James's Episcopal Church of Oneonta, New York; the Jesuits at Le Moyne; the Northeast Synod of the Presbyterian Church; the Cambridge Center for Social Studies of the U.S. Jesuit Conference; the Patrick and Anna Cudahy Fund; the Le Moyne College Committee on Faculty Research and Development; and the Jesuit Institute at Boston College, which provided a grant to Donald Kirby for a study of the adaptability of the Values Program to other colleges and universities.

We would also like to thank Frank Haig, S.J., who was president at Le Moyne when this began, and James Finlay, S.J., for their support. The current president, Kevin O'Connell, S.J., and John W. Carlson, academic vice president and dean, are most supportive of the program as well. David Smith and Mary Jo Small of the Society for Values in Higher Education rendered invaluable assistance with the Le Moyne Values Audit in 1984.

Conceptualizing, writing, and producing this book is such an integral part of the Values Program that it is nearly impossible to determine where the program and the publication begin and end. Because of the program's unique character and its grassroots nature, it is impossible to give adequate credit to everyone. Many of our best ideas grew out of the creative conflict within our dialogue and deliberations. The eight authors are those whose contribution to the Values Program began long before the idea of doing a book was ever born, and then continued until the book was completed. These authors struggled for hundreds of hours and countless days during group sessions in 1989-1990 to conceptualize and to create this book. Every draft of every chapter was discussed, torn apart, and rewritten many times by the group.

This book is a collaborative effort; it is not a collection of separate essays. But we considered it advantageous that someone assume primary responsibility for the overall book and for each chapter. The names attached to each chapter on the Contents page reflect only the principal author(s) of that chapter. This has a been a group effort in every sense. Donald Kirby spent his sabbatical leave from Le Moyne College as Visiting Scholar at the Weston School of Theology in Cambridge, Mass., with generous support from the Jesuit Institute at Boston College. The founding director of the Values Program, he spent his sabbatical steering the writing and production of this book. In an institution-wide effort such as this, it is very hard to capture how we managed to dodge the potential bureaucratic and departmental landslides and boulders that so often cause expeditions such as ours to flounder. We asked William R. Barnett to try to capture that task in his chapter. The reasons for the authorship of the other chapters will become evident as the reader progresses.

Four of the contributors to the book, two faculty members and two students, endow the book with a most unique perspective. Paul de Vries refers to that uniqueness as the program's "most potent quality," describing it as the *incarnation* of values "in the educational process." We first met Dr. de Vries when Patricia Ward, dean of Arts and Sciences at Wheaton College (Illinois), conceived the idea of an exchange between the values programs at Wheaton and Le Moyne. Each college exchanged faculty and students for three days. The exchange was so successful that we asked Paul to give us an outsider's view of the program. While de Vries was able to articulate this uniqueness, we think Robert J. Kelly's personal perspective chapter (running side by side with William Miller's) aptly catches what the Values Program does to a faculty member, his networks, and his teaching and professional skills. Kelly also volunteered to help create, fund, and administer the 1990 Summer Institute on families and public policy. So, too, with the students, David McCallum, Jr. (Le M '90) and Alison Molea (Le M '91), and their many unnamed associates in student life. McCallum directed the first student Values Committee, and in that sense is a real pioneer in our efforts to work with students. If these students and their friends had not caught the vision behind our program and been willing to sacrifice hours from their other important student duties and needs, this project would have been nothing but what Parker J. Palmer calls "a vague and airy term."

It requires a rare expertise and temperament to edit, cut, and reorganize a collaborative project so that everything fits together. Fortunately for us, David T. Lloyd, assistant professor of English and director of Le Moyne's Writing Center, possesses these qualities. Without his professional yet always understanding, critical judgment, we would never have been able to produce this manuscript.

Among the many who helped along the way, Robert Heyer, editor of Sheed & Ward, gave important advice on the shaping of the manuscript and advised us on ways to adapt the project to a wider variety of institutions. We also are particularly grateful to Frank Duesel, former director of alumni relations at Le Moyne, who first suggested that this project might be fundable, as well as to Roy Drake, S.J., Kurt Moore, Joyce Barnett, and Richard Merriman for their expert help in grantswriting. We thank J. Barron Boyd, Mary Maleski, and Fernando Salas, S.J., who read various drafts of the manuscript. Finally, our special gratitude goes to those who worked to prepare the text and related materials: Sharyn Knight, Julie Miller, Susan MacKay, Carole Beckman, Nancy Canavan, Maryann DiMichele, and Joan Mattes. If the quality of our undertaking is in any way commensurate with the quality of those who have aided us along the way, then we are fortunate indeed.

John W. Langdon

Introduction

1

Ambitious Dreams

Brian Andrews, age twenty and a junior, majors in business-finance at a private liberal arts college on the east coast. He grew up in a healthy, caring family environment where being successful and contributing to the wider community are important values. Brian's father held numerous creative administration and training positions in government and worked extensively with affirmative action programs. His mother was active on the school board. During a holiday dinner to which the family invited me, Brian remarked that minority students on his campus were given preferential treatment in tuition, living costs, scholarships, tutors, counselors, and academic advisors. He then argued that no student should receive such special treatment. (Brian himself was on a full-tuition scholarship and had recently asked me to contact a friend in Washington, D.C., about a summer job.) Brian mentioned one student in particular, Odetta Jones, who received benefits not because of merit but because of her minority status. The daughter of a single mother who supported her children by cleaning homes, Odetta had grown up in a very poor community.

One of the guests, a medical social worker at a large central city hospital, asked Brian if he and Odetta had begun college with the same opportunities. With no hesitation and some anger, Brian replied, "Yes, we're equals, and it's not fair that that black girl upstairs in our dorm should be treated differently than any other student."

I returned from that dinner disturbed: Brian's comments challenged many of my assumptions and expectations about my work as a college teacher. I began recalling questions formulated by Sharon Parks concerning the relationship between values and education: "Can moral vision and moral leadership be taught to young adults? And if so, can those characteristics be sustained across the adult years?"[1] Why, I wondered, was Brian not willing to concede that someone of Odetta's background deserved preferential treatment? Suddenly, I realized there was a large part of Brian I did not know. I wondered if I or anyone could ever reach that part of him or of any person.

Brian's observation about those less materially or educationally fortunate than himself could be construed as nothing more than a young person's flippancy. His perspective, however, cries out for a deeper understanding. I witnessed part of Brian's struggle to give meaning to the myriad, disparate experiences of his life—a struggle as deep and old as the human species itself. In his own way, Brian was building a roadbed for those life-supporting rails we call values, those guides "that keep a train on the track and help it to move smoothly, quickly, purposefully."[2] Brian's comments revealed a young man in the process of fashioning his identity. His search is at the same time unique and universal. It is, in fact, a modern version of the liberal arts and sciences' quest for unity and truth. Though the term was never used, our dinner discussion dealt with values.[3]

Brian will spend four years in a college environment—but will he develop that integrated pattern of belief and reflective philosophy of life that is the raison d'être of a liberal arts education? Most educators believe there is a need to awaken today's career-oriented students to the experience of liberal education and revitalize their commitments to social responsibility. But how can educators shape institutions so that students develop an awareness of and sensitivity to values issues? And when awareness develops, how can they teach, in Sharon Parks' words, "the formation and sustenance of moral courage,"[4] the willingness to act on values and beliefs? Those are the two main questions this book addresses.

It is because of students like Brian Andrews and Odetta Jones that members of the Le Moyne College Values Group embarked on a journey into the uncharted waters of values education. There are two visions of what values education involves. The first, often perceived as proselytizing, promotes the transmission of specific values content. The second attempts to enhance students' ability to analyze and reflect on values issues, so that they eventually strengthen and deepen their own values framework. The Le Moyne Values Program supports the second vision: we hope to help students fashion a defensible and consistent values framework, one that does not collapse under life's pressures and psychological stresses. Our project does not transmit or inculcate a specific set of values; we have created an idea and a process, not a rigid program.

We chose the term "values education" rather than "moral education" or "ethics education" to reflect our concern with a wide range of human values. Its broader orientation makes the term "values education" potentially relevant to every aspect of academic life. It includes values analysis, values consciousness, values criticism, values pedagogy, and values development.[5] If our only concern were to teach "ethics," the challenge would not be so great. But, to quote Sharon Parks again, it is, "challenging indeed in an age of profound cultural transition to help students develop *moral courage*—the power to create and then act upon one's finest understanding of the public good."[6]

In the past three decades, changes in society, national life, and education have produced or been accompanied by changes in religion and patterns of belief. How, in this dynamic context, can educators best exercise their mission? Although the Le Moyne Values Group cannot presume to answer this question for everyone, we are convinced that our experience speaks to issues shared by many in higher education. A number of educators have described and analyzed the problem of values illiteracy, but to our knowledge no one has developed an interactive, college-wide process or program. We have at least made a beginning, identifying the need for values education and creating a simple and effective plan.

Two events provided the original impetus for the Le Moyne College Values Program. The first occurred in 1984, when Le Moyne became one of eight educational institutions nationwide to undertake "values audits" as part of a pilot project sponsored by the Society for Values in Higher Education. Through its values audit, each institution diagnosed the implicit assumptions that mold its culture and consequently its policies and decisions. Participating institutions hoped to increase their self-awareness and survivability—and then to become pilot projects for other institutions addressing similar concerns. In addition to Le Moyne, participating institutions were Susquehanna University; the University of Tennessee, Knoxville; Centre College, Kentucky; California State at Long Beach; the University of Wisconsin, Green Bay; Willamette University; and Southwest Texas State.

Under the aegis of the Values Audit, the Le Moyne Values Group began to diagnose gaps between the college's assertions and its realities. We sought to identify values and conflicts in three areas: the Jesuit tradition at Le Moyne College, the governance of the college, and the college's educational enterprise as a whole, especially its student life component. Our internal Values Audit disclosed a need for the college to develop a "deepened awareness of its communal values" as a vehicle "to guide the college as it makes decisions crucial to its future." It caused some in the college to become conscious of a dissonance between what the college said it was and did and what it really was and really did. And it highlighted the fact that students at Le Moyne—as at most other liberal arts colleges in this country—were becoming increasingly vocational and insulated.

The second impetus was our 1985 core revision process. Our "Core Curriculum Evaluation Report" stressed that "one of the essential features of the revised core should be the constant encouraging of students . . . to explore the connections that courses have with each other and with life outside academics." It further emphasized that "core courses are intended to be instrumental in helping students to shape their attitudes and values."

The Values Audit and the core curriculum revision process cleared the air, allowing faculty members to put forward tough questions which could be discussed without rancor or personal conflict. People who had retreated into their closed offices began to come out; new life percolated throughout the campus. We acknowledged the dissonance between image and reality and began to wonder how unique that dissonance was to Le Moyne College. So when the director of alumni relations asked if I would be interested in applying to a foundation for a small seed grant to examine some of the issues raised by the Values Audit and curriculum reform, I agreed. Within days the proposal was in the mail. During the summer we received word from the Raskob Foundation that Le Moyne would receive $5,000 to create a seminar designed to help students integrate their professional interests with the college's liberal arts tradition.

This first grant provided a small stipend for a group of six faculty and one administrator to convene for one year. We were tenured faculty in business administration and law, history, political science, religious studies, and psychology. The administrator was the director of admissions. The "Working Group on Values" (as we called ourselves) created a year-long seminar in which some widely distributed reports on the deficiencies of higher education and *Habits of the Heart* by Robert Bellah, et al., served as the tools for our discussions. These readings confirmed that what we had perceived at Le Moyne was actually much larger in scope. We came to realize that a single seminar or series of seminars would touch only a few faculty and students and would thus fail to confront the extensive problems we had examined.

One problem is rampant vocationalism. The students we teach at Le Moyne manifest an especially strong career orientation, which translates into an overwhelming drive to become certified for a particular career so as to get a job and make money. And that careerism has intensified over the last decade. Whereas in 1980 freshmen would admit with some embarrassment that they attended college to prepare for making "as much money as possible," by 1987 they were proud of such a reply. We began to understand that we must engage students in issues and skills beyond their ordinary concerns. We began to see afresh that our students have difficulty making connections between what they learn in college and their lives after college. More specifically, we addressed our growing apprehension that a college education no longer enables undergraduates to develop those integrated patterns of belief which are so vital to constructive participation in society. Our challenge was to discover how we might awaken today's career-oriented students to the full potential of a liberal arts education—and thus revitalize their commitment to social responsibility.

Le Moyne's program was created to meet this challenge by promoting a college-wide awareness of and sensitivity to values issues. Since we did not know how to begin such a large project, we looked about for appropriate models—but soon found there were none. We then decided to create a model on our own, borrowing parts and pieces from other institutions. The Values Audit had noted that any change in the college's perception of the role of values would require "the efforts and commitment of the entire community, especially the faculty, and an unqualified commitment of time, money, and energy from the top level administrators over a considerable period of time (3-5 years)." The report stressed that "anything less—a one-shot program involving the entire community or a program involving one or two faculty or administrative offices—will be shrugged off by the institution as a whole." We did not need an isolated program— there were already many of these; what we needed was a program involving the entire community in as many ways as possible. The result was our Values Program, a program in process. Early on we defined two broad goals. The first was to make a major impact on values education and development at Le Moyne; the second was to help create an institution where this kind of learning was possible. In 1987 we returned to the Raskob Foundation for a second grant to try to make our ambitious dream a reality.

The second Raskob Foundation grant allowed the Working Group on Values to meet regularly to discuss issues we felt were most pressing on our campus. Among the issues was the tension between individualism and social commitment, as treated in *Habits of the Heart*. Bellah's team concluded that individualism, rather than equality of opportunity, is the dominant force in American history, and that the triumph of this ethos has resulted in declining community values. As Donald Swift asserts, "In a society where the individualist ethos is supreme, relationships are built on giving and getting and are inevitably fragile and impermanent. It is necessary 'to go along to get along' in the workplace to obtain the wherewithal to purchase our private pleasures."[7] These kinds of concerns and attitudes have weakened the normative values of church, family, and neighborhood.

A second issue the Values Group addressed was the status of faculty. The college expected a faculty member to be a superb teacher, a superb researcher, and readily available for students and committees. The college reward structure, however, placed primary emphasis on the importance of research and publication. This disparity between what the school claimed to reward and what it actually rewarded caused relentless anxiety.

At Le Moyne College the faculty constitute less of a community than even a decade ago. Some faculty, preoccupied by individual professional pursuits, have become increasingly linked to national or international networks of specialists in their own disciplines rather than to colleagues and activities at the local institution. Their professional identity is attached more closely to an academic discipline than to the role of teaching professor. Other faculty, heavily engaged in campus activities, governance, and teaching, see their identities tied to the life of the college. As mentioned, the reward structure for faculty increasingly favors those who publish and so encourages identification with one's discipline rather than one's college. Our group began to question whether we as a faculty or an institution would be able to function effectively if this separation into two distinct classes defined faculty relations at our college.

Today, few members of the academic community share the same values and interests, and many faculty feel they are becoming powerless before administrators who want to run the college according to plans developed by an increasingly complex bureaucracy. Not only are faculty more diverse and cosmopolitan than ever before, but colleges and universities are adopting organizational frameworks similar to those in industry and business. Financial aid sources, for example, can exert a tremendous influence on an evolving college. As public and private monies for student financial aid arrive, they are accompanied by policies, offices, and staff. Grants and contracts bring another set of requirements. Such external forms of coercion can create elaborate bureaucratic structures while shifting power from the faculty to the growing administrative core.[8]

How do these issues affect the students? A young person en-
rolled in a college brings with her concrete cultural orientations
imbued since birth. These orientations are not just ideas but
also "habits of the heart"; they are the lived story of the
American people—their basic commitment and orienting identity. Because these commitments are embedded in and
incorporated into their ways of living, it is their philosophy and
theology. Our experience with the values audit convinced us
that these orientations of the larger environment and society
also are deeply structured and embedded in institutions. A college is one of those institutions, one of those recurring patterns
of cooperations among peoples, or stated more simply, the ways
people behave. We had begun to recognize that we needed to attend not only to the faculty, staff, and students, but to the institution itself.

As I write, on leave from Le Moyne, I sit overlooking a major
university with many departments in separate buildings, each
with its own requirements. In this environment there can be little university-wide sense about what students should study. I
am reminded of the bright junior at a prestigious state research
university who expressed to me his frustration that he was allowed to drift from course to course for his first two years with
little or no supervision. There do not seem to be many instances
of professors or students utilizing university-wide resources. (Of
course, even small liberal arts colleges cannot guarantee integration. A department chair at one such institution advises his
majors, "take the easy teachers for your core requirements but
excel in the toughest of the bread-and-butter courses.") For some
students, this fragmentation makes the purpose of the college
years very clear: choose a career, then prepare for that career.

Turning to the classroom, another knotty question arises: Is
there such a thing as a values-free education? The professionalism of graduate school makes many teachers fearful of
dealing with values in the classroom. They face a flurry of difficult questions: Are all positions of equal value? Should
teachers admit their feelings or beliefs about an issue to students? Should teachers respond differently according to whether
their students are predominantly Catholic, Jewish, Protestant,
or Muslim? How does one deal with the prejudices of his or her

own discipline? How does one acknowledge that one's college may have a different founding purpose than others?

In my senior seminar on "Corporate Responsibility," I am always surprised at how soon the senior has become the accountant, biologist, or historian. By age twenty-one she already carries the attitudes, language, and thought patterns of her teachers and models. In this course, students soon come to realize that their various fields are in competition and often promote opposing values. For the first time, some students see stark differences among value systems. I increasingly sense in students a deep need for insights into values. Graduating seniors are often frustrated—they want to do the right thing, but they don't know how.

Many of those involved in education wonder whether members of college or university communities should accept the responsibility to promote values. This question points to the fear that a small group or an entire college will impose its beliefs on impressionable young minds and hearts. The Values Group agrees that no one person, group, or institution should impose its values on anyone. But strong value positions are already being subtly communicated to students and parents by the courses, the professors, the sports programs and dormitory lifestyles available, the requirements demanded, and the rewards and promotions offered. By ignoring the fact that, however indirectly, all institutions and systems already impose their values, this question fudges crucial issues.

Another question is whether values education should be the exclusive province of parents, families, and religious groups. But these institutions, which traditionally transmitted societal mores, have lost much of their influence. While we are not denying that parents and other caretakers have responsibility, we also believe educators share that responsibility. Students are going to live and work in our colleges and universities for four years. We need to discover how best to serve those who, during these formative years, will in any case absorb the values inherent in all colleges and universities. While students are attending our educational institutions, we have a responsibility to address their needs.

At the heart of all these questions is a single question: How does one respect the professional and personal freedom of the student, professor, and university while arguing that people need to commit themselves to some form of truth, to some specific worldview or set of values?

In response to the issues described above, our group set out to create a prototypical, two-year program promoting values education at the college level. Our approach called for a community effort consisting of two interactive components: the Summer Institute and the Academic Forum. Integral to both would be ongoing research and evaluation. We advocated a college-wide approach to engage students fully and demonstrate how values issues affect all realms of life. The college years, after all, account for only 7% of students' lives, and out of the 168 hours in a week, only 15 are spent in the classroom. We wanted our interactive program to present a total environment for values learning.

The first dimension of the program, the Summer Institute, is the component concerned with faculty development. Given the critical role the faculty plays in values education, we recognized the importance of beginning the program with them. The Summer Institute is organized around a particular values-laden theme (for example, economic justice). Through consideration of this theme, participants seek to understand the role of values education across the curriculum and gain experience in pedagogical techniques that encourage students to reflect upon their values. Participants include administrators as well as faculty since both groups must work together to create an environment which nurtures values education. Chapters 2 and 3 of this book describe the first two Summer Institutes, which focused on the themes of economic justice and peace and war, respectively.

The second dimension of the program, the Academic Forum, discussed in chapter 4, coordinates with the Summer Institute around a common theme each year. Consisting of a series of lectures, panels, films, theatrical presentations, library and art exhibits, student discussions, faculty colloquia, and other events, the Academic Forum focuses campus extracurricular activities on a significant year-long theme. Each separate group (the Women's History Week Committee or the Accounting Club, for example), is encouraged to create and sponsor events related to the theme, thereby coordinating the out-of-classroom experience so that students of all majors are more receptive to the values issues raised in their courses. The Summer Institute and Academic Forum enable students and faculty to bring newly acquired knowledge, materials, and enthusiasm to the classroom. In a similar way, our essay and art contest helps integrate papers and assignments, both artistic and academic, during the year.

The Academic Forum interacts with the Summer Institute. The idea of students bringing newly acquired knowledge and enthusiasm to the classroom experience, moreover, dovetails nicely with the faculty's utilization of new materials and approaches on the same coordinating theme. Based on the integrating theme of each year, the Forum focuses the attention of the college community on issues to which liberal education speaks with profundity and wisdom. The theme is extended to other aspects of student life, such as freshman orientation, parent's weekend, college liturgical celebrations, dorm tutorials, weekend retreat workshops for campus leaders, and workshops run by the placement office to increase student awareness of life options involving public service.

While Part One of this volume outlines the program's components, Part Two, Personal Reflections, describes how these components affected some participants. Bob Kelly and Bill Miller, who took part in the 1988 Summer Institute, relate their experiences in chapters 5 and 6, respectively. David McCallum and Alison Molea, two students involved in implementing the Academic Forum, express their perspectives in chapter 7.

It is beyond the scope of this introduction to describe the process of how we acquired the commitment of the faculty, the administration, and the larger community—a critical issue for the viability of transforming the ethos of the college. Chapter 8 discusses how that commitment was achieved and how we then were able to strike a balance—in an age of limited resources—between our needs and the needs of other college programs.

Chapter 9 discusses ongoing empirical evaluation and research. The evaluation element helps Institute participants develop an agenda of specific issues, goals, and means to achieve goals. It also assists the Values Group in determining the Institute's overall success as well as in assessing the effectiveness of specific features. While the evaluation element focuses on Institute Fellows, the research effort assesses faculty and student attitudes toward values issues in the classroom. It also helps determine the extent to which faculty use the classroom to assist students in becoming conscious of the valuation element of their decision making. To date, three questionnaires (one to survey faculty, one to survey students, and one to survey first semester freshmen) have been distributed. These surveys measure beliefs about the overall role of values education, the curriculum's perceived impact on students and values, the relationship between pedagogy and values, and the impact of Academic Forum activities on student sensitivity to values.

This book does not sound an alarm about "values illiteracy"; that alarm has already been sounded by others. Rather, its purpose is to speak to those who feel deeply and think often about values issues but remain isolated. Our audience is any person or group influenced by or influential in the educational process. More specifically, we speak to those working at colleges and universities. We would like to address teachers who have already tried certain steps, e.g., incorporating values issues within a course or developing ethics programs for schools. (Chapter 10, by Paul de Vries of Wheaton College, gives a perspective on the program from a faculty member at another institution.) The method, goal, and technique of this volume are closely related: we intend to get readers to imagine a process, to be enthused about the idea, and to consider whether and in what ways they can undertake a similar project.

The Values Program is worth considering because it correlates with a distinctive concept of liberal learning, one that taps into many underutilized college resources. It discusses how liberal arts education can be reinvigorated through an approach that deals not just with the humanities or curriculum in general, but also with the entire institution, including areas of student life, development, and admissions.

This volume is not a definitive analysis. Rather, it provides an introduction to a values program, an informal discussion of its elements and impacts. The goals of this program should be quite clear by now. We want to increase values sensitivity, to educate students in values-related skills, and to connect what students learn during their education with how they live after graduation. This program is different from others in that it is institution-wide, involving faculty, students, administrators, and staff—virtually every aspect of the academic community.

Values are learned. When a society teaches that individual goals have priority over civic responsibility, that society is in peril. Our program advocates education for civic responsibility and personal virtue. Students need to exercise moral courage, and our approach argues that there is hope: there is a way to accomplish values education in a pluralistic framework.

Endnotes

1. Sharon Daloz Parks, "Ethics, Commerce and Theological Education: Reflections While Walking Across the River," *News From Weston* X.1 (1989): 1. See the development of her ideas in *The Critical Years: The Young Adult's Search for Meaning, Faith, and Commitment* (New York: Harper & Row, 1990).

2. From Peter-Hans Kolvenbach, S.J., "What a Marvelous Opportunity for the Magis," an address given at "Assembly 1989: Jesuit Ministry in Higher Education," June 7, Georgetown University. The printed text appeared in the *National Jesuit News* 18:10 (1989).

3. In this paragraph and elsewhere I am indebted to Sharon Parks for her description of "meaning-making" by young adults which she presents in *The Critical Years: The Young Adult's Search for Meaning, Faith, and Commitment*.

4. Parks, "Ethics, Commerce and Theological Education."

5. See Richard L. Morrill's analysis of the term "values education" in *Teaching Values in College* (San Francisco: Jossey-Bass, Inc., 1980). His work on values in education partially stimulated the Le Moyne Values Group to begin our project.

6. Parks, "Ethics, Commerce and Theological Education."

7. Donald Swift, "Perspectives: The American Heart," in *Cross Currents,* Vol. XXXVI (1986-87): 386.

8. In this and the preceding paragraph I am indebted to Richard M. Levinson's discussion of higher education in his article, "The Faculty and Institutional Isomorphism," *Academe* 75.1 (1989): 23-27.

Part One:
Program Components

2

The 1988 Summer Institute

Introduction

A group of faculty are seated around the table in the Faculty Dining Room, discussing the upcoming Summer Institute. One describes his frustrations as a teacher this way: "Whenever I lecture about topics central to the theme of my introductory course, students are busy listening attentively and taking notes. Occasionally, I try to draw them into a discussion of current events related to topics in the course, but it just doesn't work. When I attempt to initiate these discussions, most students' eyes glaze over. I then retreat to the safety of the familiar lecture. I'm hoping my participation in the Summer Institute will help me become more effective in stimulating students to think about the implications of my discipline."

This all too familiar scenario illustrates two topics which are integral to the Summer Institute—pedagogy and content. It shows the tension between lecture and discussion as methods of instruction, and it points out the perceived difference between "academic" content and the events and issues of the "real world." In a more subtle way, it also shows that the pedagogical method and the content of a course are inextricably related; the distinction between process and content is an artificial one.

The lecture method structures the process of learning in a particular way. The teacher is to be the focal point from which

19

knowledge flows. The student is to be an active listener, assimilating the essentials of what is being transmitted. The student must also weigh what is being said and determine if it makes sense in the context of his or her limited understanding of the material. If not, the student must ask questions which will evoke clarification and increased comprehension.

The discussion method promotes learning differently because the teacher is not a source of all knowledge, but a source of questions. Knowledge flows from the students, who are prompted and facilitated by the teacher. Students are both speakers and active listeners. A discussion creates an opportunity for expression of the student's own ideas, for reflection on the ideas of other students, and for reaction to the teacher's questions.

The frustrated teacher mentioned at the beginning of this chapter tried the discussion method, but it didn't work. The students' eyes "glazed over" and the teacher returned to "the safety of the familiar lecture." Why? When students "tune out" discussion, it may be because they feel that, since the course emphasizes the accumulation of content and rewards the mastery of that material, discussion is unimportant. Students may believe that, because current events are not likely to appear on a certain exam, they are therefore insignificant.

For faculty, the content of academic disciplines is contained within a clearly defined "terrain of discourse." Courses in a discipline are divided into manageable doses of content, and the teacher aims to present these in an intelligible and palatable manner. These doses of content are set out in a course outline which logically orders them and which specifies what "simply must be covered" during a semester.

It is not surprising that, after years of education structured this way, students can sense the difference between material which clearly falls within the discipline and that which does not. In a field with settled boundaries and a "terrain of discourse," current events or issues are clearly extraneous. And when the shift in content coincides with a shift from the lecture to the discussion method—shifting the focus from the teacher who "knows" the material to the students who don't—the message about the irrelevance of current material is reinforced.

The act of raising questions about the relevance of current events to course content implies that there is something problematic about the usual way of viewing academic disciplines. Saying that discussion of current events is an important part of a given course means that disciplines are open-ended. Clearly, both teacher and students must understand this in order to make meaningful reflection on current events possible.

The problem the teacher in the opening incident faces cannot be resolved simply by the adoption of a different pedagogical method, because the interaction between teacher and students is only part of the problem. Similarly, a reorganization of course content would be insufficient to resolve the problem. After all, if the teacher hopes to stimulate student thinking, careful attention must be given to methods of realizing that hope. Seeing the interconnectedness of these topics makes one aware of the artificiality of the process-content distinction. Although it will be necessary to discuss these themes separately at times, it is important to stress their interconnectedness at the outset.

The Summer Institute is that dimension of the Values Program which seeks to provide an effective strategy for dealing with the interrelated issues of pedagogy and course content. Chapter 3 will provide an in-depth look at the 1989 Summer Institute. This chapter will examine the planning process which led up to the first Summer Institute in 1988, give an account of its operation, and finally comment on its outcomes.

Planning for the First Summer Institute

As recounted in chapter 1, six faculty members and the director of admissions began meeting on a regular basis during the 1985-86 academic year to discuss the implications of the 1984 Values Audit and the ongoing core curriculum revision. Their discussions initially aimed at developing an interdisciplinary senior studies course which would enable students to reflect upon their values commitments. But the group soon realized that a single course would reach very few students. Amid the frustrations of deciding what to do, Donald Kirby, S.J., director of the group, asked group members to read and discuss *Habits of the Heart,* by Robert Bellah et al., which had been used as an effective instrument for stimulating thought about values issues at a Society for Values in Higher Education symposium. Thus, *Habits of the Heart* became a vehicle for the group to enter into a dialogue about values in the contemporary world.

The most significant consequence that emerged from these discussions was the building of community. All of the participants agreed that, although the book was flawed, their discussions built a spirit of cooperation and trust that held the group together during the next two difficult years of grant-writing. The interaction was excellent. There was a sense of playing with ideas and feeling free to challenge others—everyone felt this give-and-take to be useful. Although one might be tempted to call any group of faculty who meet regularly for a specified purpose a committee, the intellectual delight these individuals experienced was decidedly uncommittee-like. Fr. Kirby wisely let the group follow its own pace with no apparent end in view other than the intrinsic value of enlightened conversation. Anyone who hopes to replicate the essentials of this project must provide sufficient time and a congenial setting in which faculty planning the program can come to know one another and develop a sense of trust in one another. Clearly, if this process had not occurred at Le Moyne College, a viable Values Program would not have been achieved.

By the end of the 1985-86 academic year, the group had progressed far beyond the idea of developing a single interdisciplinary course and had begun to think about what might be done to exert a more substantial impact upon the life of the college. Fr. Kirby had secured an additional grant from the Raskob Foundation to support the group's activity for the following academic year. In September 1986, the Consortium for the Advancement of Private Higher Education (CAPHE) invited Le Moyne College to present a funding proposal. The college administration then asked the Values Group to develop the proposal, thus changing the group's agenda from a leisurely discussion of future possibilities to focused work on an immediate project.

Since the deadline for submitting the CAPHE proposal was set for mid-November, acceptance of the invitation meant committing the group to developing a strategy for values education. The group, however, faced two major obstacles: there was no grantsperson in the development office at the time, and the college had no significant history of institutional grant applications for academic purposes. To address these obstacles, the group decided to bring in two outside consultants who had grant-writing experience. With their assistance, the group formulated a request for a matching grant of $50,000 which would support one key element in the Values Program: the Summer Institute. In March 1987, the Values Group received notification that CAPHE had approved the matching grant proposal.

Planning for the first Summer Institute began with the writing of the CAPHE grant proposal. To understand the Summer Institute's role in our plan for values education, let us begin with an examination of the CAPHE proposal.

The overall goal for the Summer Institute, as enunciated in the proposal, was to "develop specific strategies and methodologies for incorporating values education across the curriculum." In the eyes of the group, values education should not be considered the sole responsibility of the philosophy and religious studies departments, or even the humanities. Rather, values education can become part of the mission of any college department. This point was stressed in the proposal's assertion that "particular attention would be given to involving 'objective content' (e.g. mathematics, foreign language, science, accounting) with normative considerations." Why are foreign language and science included in the list of examples of what the proposal calls 'objective content?' The vast majority of students study a foreign language in order to fulfill a requirement of their major. The courses they take are primarily language, as opposed to literature, courses. One then wonders whether a course devoted to the structural elements of a foreign language can include a values component.

As far as science is concerned, courses such as bioethics can fruitfully raise values questions in the context of scientific inquiry. However, science courses taught to undergraduate majors tend not to include these questions. Although the myth that scientific inquiry is value-free has been effectively shattered, many practicing scientists still act as if it were true. This attitude carries over into the classroom.

To achieve the overall goal of incorporating values education across the curriculum, two features would have to become part of the plan. First, it would be necessary to recruit faculty for the Summer Institute from as wide an array of academic departments as possible. The group agreed that the Summer Institute would include about twenty faculty members. That size would allow for diversity and yet maintain sufficient intimacy for the purposes of interaction. Second, stress would be placed upon the development of pedagogical techniques which Institute participants could utilize in their courses and which would integrate values education into their disciplines in meaningful and exciting ways. Participants would have the opportunity to meet in small groups and share ideas about teaching practices with colleagues from both allied and diverse disciplines. This was seen as an ideal way of drawing upon the collective pedagogical experience and wisdom of the faculty in a non-threatening and supportive context.

As can be seen thus far, the group placed a good deal of importance upon the development of sound pedagogical techniques. But such development could not take place in a vacuum. It was necessary to give careful thought to the selection of topics for the first two Summer Institutes because the group knew that the topic would have to be sufficiently attractive for faculty to be willing to attend the Summer Institute. After all, since their professional lives are tied to the content of their disciplines, the prospect of an extended discussion of pedagogical techniques alone would not merit serious consideration. After lengthy reflection alone upon the history of Le Moyne College as a Roman Catholic and a Jesuit institution, the group decided it would be appropriate for members of the college community to reflect upon the issues raised in the two pastoral letters issued by the United States bishops in the last decade—economic justice and peace. Economic justice would be the theme of the first Summer Institute, and peace and war the theme of the second.

To establish credibility for the Summer Institute among the faculty, the group thought it important for outside facilitators to run the Summer Institute. Because we adopted a traditional process-content distinction, we saw the need for two facilitators, one whose strength matched the Institute's theme and the other whose strength was tied to the process of educating. The distinction, though theoretically sharp, blurred in practice. The facilitators, after all, were educators, and no strong educator can be concerned solely with either process or content.

One piece of advice the group received from CAPHE regarding the writing of the proposal concerned the identification of facilitators. Although it seemed strange to name the facilitators for the first Summer Institute some twenty months in advance, we proceeded to consult sources, both on and off campus, to arrive at a short list of prospects. We then sought commitments from two nationally known figures who tentatively agreed to serve as facilitators. They were Dr. Richard Morrill and Dr. Kenneth Dolbeare. Dr. Morrill, then president of Centre College and currently president at the University of Richmond, is the author of *Teaching Values in College* and has served as lecturer, consultant, and workshop leader on values and liberal education at over thirty conferences, colleges, and universities since 1981. Dr. Kenneth Dolbeare, professor of Political Science at Evergreen State College, is the author of *Democracy at Risk: The Politics of Economic Renewal and American Public Policy: A Citizen's Guide*. The group originally thought that Dr. Morrill would be the facilitator primarily responsible for content, and Dr. Dolbeare would be the process person.

The group established a set of ambitious objectives for the Summer Institute. The participants were to

1. become familiar with the literature on values formation;

2. become acquainted with the literature on the theme of the Academic Forum;

3. have a better understanding of the place of values in the classroom relationship;

4. experience pedagogical techniques addressing the issue of values in course content;

5. plan course modifications within their usual teaching assignment so as to permit treatment of values.

These ambitious objectives presumed that much could be accomplished in three weeks, indicating the high level of expectation group members had for this critical phase of faculty development.

Slowly our strategy for values education was falling into place. We had conceived an idea for a Summer Institute, decided our objectives, and chosen our facilitators. Next we set the dates for the 1988 Summer Institute. The group decided that three weeks in June would be best. That would leave three weeks between the end of the spring semester and the beginning of the Institute for participants to engage in intensive preparation. Since the Institute would coincide with a substantial portion of the first summer school session, the participants would be paid a stipend roughly equivalent to teaching one summer course.

The first problem arose when we contacted the facilitators. Initially, the group wanted the Institute to begin on Monday, June 6. But graduation at Centre College, where Dr. Morrill was president, was scheduled for June 5. In addition, Dr. Morrill was preparing to move from Centre College to the University of Richmond and would be able to spend only two days at the Institute. Thus, it became necessary to initiate a search for a third facilitator. The group remained committed to Dr. Morrill's presence at the Institute, however brief it might be, because of his extensive workshop experience related to the first objective—values formation. What seemed to be a problem was actually an opportunity. The group had already given some thought to selecting someone familiar with the evolution of the U.S. bishops' pastoral letter on economic justice. After a lengthy search, the group was fortunate to add Professor John Langan, S.J., Rose Kennedy Professor of Christian Ethics at Georgetown University, as a third facilitator. Fr. Langan would be unable to attend the first week of the Institute because of previous commitments. Although the situation was less than ideal, it was hoped that Dr. Dolbeare would be effective in coordinating the transition from Dr. Morrill to Fr. Langan.

The next element in planning was the choice of participants from the Le Moyne faculty. The group decided to have faculty apply for the twenty places and to designate those selected as CAPHE Fellows. A simple, one-page application form was developed and sent to all full-time faculty members. Applicants were asked to list the courses they taught. Then they were asked to describe what they expected to gain as a result of participation in the Summer Institute and what they could contribute to the sessions. We set forth three major criteria for selection. First, we hoped to attract a substantial group of senior faculty. If the Institute proved successful, senior faculty would become influential agents for change in their departments. Second, we sought as diverse a representation of departments as possible because we believed that values education had to be spread throughout the curriculum to become effective. Finally, the applications themselves would be reviewed in order to select motivated and enthusiastic participants. Nineteen participants, representing thirteen departments, were chosen.

The final and crucial element of planning involved the determination of what would go on during the three weeks of the Summer Institute. For this to occur, the facilitators would have to be brought together to become more fully conversant with the objectives of the Institute and shape the program's structure accordingly. Since the decision to add Fr. Langan as a third facilitator was not made until late January of 1988, and since the schedules of the facilitators were already crowded by then, it was impossible to find a common time for a meeting. I arranged a meeting with Dr. Dolbeare and Fr. Langan in March.

Dr. Dolbeare and Fr. Langan decided to have Dr. Morrill organize the first two days of the Institute. After reviewing the applications of those selected to participate and the objectives of the Summer Institute, they discussed how best to structure the ten remaining days. They suggested three questions as a way of focusing the energies of the participants. Given our status as faculty at a Jesuit college and citizens of the United States in the closing years of the twentieth century, the first question would be: Who are we, economically and morally? Dr. Dolbeare would speak on the topic of the coherence of the world we live in; and the text, *Habits of the Heart,* would focus discussion. The second question would be: How did we come to be the way we are? Readings for this segment of the Institute would include selections from *The Federalist Papers,* Marx's *Communist Manifesto*, and Joseph Schumpeter's *Capitalism, Socialism, and Democracy*.

The final question would be future-directed and international in scope: What should we do about economic justice? The readings appropriate to this question would be the U.S. bishops' pastoral letter, *Economic Justice for All,* Lawrence Goodwyn's *The Populist Moment,* and *The Pedagogy of the Oppressed* by Paolo Freire.

The group invited Dr. Morrill to campus during the 1988 spring semester to share in a public celebration of what was to begin in the summer by delivering the keynote address entitled "Educating for Values." While on campus, he met with the Values Group to offer encouragement for their efforts to advance values education, and with interested students to stimulate their enthusiasm for the 1988-89 Academic Forum on economic justice. He also discussed his plans for the first two days of the Institute and agreed to provide selected articles which would address three topics: theories of moral development and their pedagogical implications, values and the process of inquiry, and the use of ethical theory in applied ethics. Finally, he spoke with the incoming Institute participants about their concerns. First, the participants sought some assurance that the amount of required reading would not be too great. This would allow participants to suggest additional readings. Second, the schedule should be flexible enough to permit both exploration of ideas arising from discussion and individual conferences with the facilitators. Finally, some time should be built into the schedule to consider pedagogical techniques which would enable participants to introduce the theme of economic justice into their courses in a natural way. These concerns were communicated to Dr. Dolbeare and Fr. Langan, who subsequently adjusted the reading list.

The Summer Institute

Recall the incident recounted at the beginning of this chapter. For that faculty member's concern to be addressed, it would be necessary to avoid turning the Summer Institute into something like a National Endowment for the Humanities (NEH) summer seminar. What was called for was not a profound insight into the essence of economic justice, but an understanding of the relationship of economic justice to one's discipline and some facility in communicating this relationship to students. Since the participants represented thirteen different disciplines, a good deal of the responsibility for achieving our objectives would fall upon them. The facilitators were themselves representatives of distinct disciplines and could not be expected to resolve the concerns of participants from other disciplines. Indeed the role of facilitators was to do no more than set the context for group inquiry and stimulate individual inquiry.

In the eyes of the participants, the first Summer Institute turned out to be a uniquely positive learning experience. (See chapter 9 for more details.) I shall attempt to communicate the nature of that experience through a chronological account and interpretation of the flow of events and activities during the three weeks of the Institute. The focus for each week's activities is reflected in the keynote question at the beginning of the subsections.

Week One:
Who are we, economically and morally?

The Summer Institute began on Wednesday, June 8. The participants gathered to hear the president of Le Moyne College officially open the Institute. Dr. Richard Morrill began the first session with a review of the major contributions of Lawrence Kohlberg to moral development theory. Kohlberg argues that one must go through three stages of cognitive development to achieve moral maturity. These are the preconventional stage (where the conventions of society have not profoundly affected one's thinking), the conventional stage (where one's thought reflects social conventions), and the postconventional stage (where one's thinking goes beyond the limits of social convention).[1] After discussing the intellectual sources of Kohlberg's ideas, Dr. Morrill involved the group in a consideration of "Heinz's dilemma," a case used by Kohlberg and his associates to determine an individual's stage of moral development. This led to an examination of the limitations of Kohlberg's theory. The work of Carol Gilligan was cited as one critique of these limitations. Gilligan argues that Kohlberg's empirical research, which used only males as subjects, is not valid for depicting female moral development.[2]

The next session was devoted to the teaching of ethics. Dr. Morrill began with an account of the recent efforts of philosophers and theologians to develop the domain of applied normative ethics and, more particularly, professional ethics. The group then reflected upon and discussed selected cases in an effort to gain some appreciation for the ethical dimensions of human problems. These two sessions convinced participants that to engage in values education one must understand one's own stage of moral development as well as that of one's students.

Dr. Morrill next focused the group's attention upon major themes raised in his book, *Teaching Values in College.* The first theme was the meaning of the term, "values." If we understand values as standards of choice guiding persons and groups toward fulfillment, we can then see the act of valuing as a part of ordinary experience. The next theme concerned the implications of this understanding of values for educational practice. Educating for values requires the development of analytical and critical abilities. As educators, we are committed to those values which are fundamental to the existence of any educational community. Part of our task is to encourage students to subject their own system of values to careful analysis and criticism.

With this understanding of values education as a background, the participants began to discuss *Habits of the Heart.* They agreed that significant characteristics of culture in the United States surfaced in the book. They recognized that, as products of this culture, they had to come to terms with such qualities as excessive individualism and the consequent fragility of community. Thus, any effort to understand stages of moral development would have to be set in the context of life and culture in the United States in the closing years of the twentieth century.

With the completion of Dr. Morrill's contribution, Dr. Kenneth Dolbeare assumed direction of the group. There were two items on his agenda: completion of the discussion of *Habits of the Heart,* and a discussion of how best to use the time left in the next two weeks. Professor Dolbeare distributed a sheet entitled, "Shaping the Agenda: Values and Economic Justice," which set forth the conclusions of the March planning meeting. The group discussed the need to come to terms with each of the topics. The first topic was the question of who we are and how we came to be the way we are. As white, middle-class American professionals, we carry with us intellectual and social baggage which needs to be examined. The second topic raised the issue of what, as educators, we propose to do about values and economic justice. Responding to this issue requires an understanding of the nature of education and the context in which we act as educators. Thus, we have to know something about American education and the institutional goals of education at Le Moyne College.

The third topic reflected the need to conceptualize our relationship to the problem of economic justice. Dr. Dolbeare argued that politics and economics must be viewed as connected, and that political economy is a mostly coherent, evolving system. It is important for us to examine selected moments in the history of political economy to understand our roles as products and creators of this evolving system. We are in a period of transformation, and the U.S. bishops' pastoral letter is best understood as an effort to address this transformation. The final topic concerned strategies for achieving our goals as educators, given an understanding of the present context of political economy. An effort must be made to address the question of integrating content and method in our courses. At the close, Dr. Dolbeare suggested that at the beginning of the next week the group attempt to arrive at some consensus about what would be done during the remaining days of the Institute. As the first week ended, participants went their separate ways, charged with the task of setting the agenda for the next two weeks.

Dr. Dolbeare introduced two significant changes during the first week. First, he reorganized the physical arrangement of the meeting room from chairs arranged in rows facing a lectern to tables and chairs arranged in a square. As a result, participants were able to interact with one another more effectively. Second, he shifted the responsibility for setting the agenda from the facilitators to the participants. As we shall see, these changes transformed the character of the Institute.

Week Two:
How did we come to be the way we are?

The second week of the Institute began with the introduction of Father John Langan, S.J., to the participants. The topic for the first session was "Ethics in a Business Setting." After giving a brief description of his activity as a director of workshops for Chemical Bank executives, Fr. Langan presented a case involving a possible decision to close a branch office of a bank in an economically depressed community. He then divided the participants into groups representing the various interests relevant to this decision (e.g. the State Banking Commission, the local bank manager, the mayor). After some time for preparation, the participants conducted a mock hearing in an effort to arrive at a decision regarding the branch closing. The exchange among the participants was lively and creative. The group then discussed a staff reduction case in which a supervisor of a department had to choose one employee out of seven for a layoff. Key issues considered were: (1) Is there any sound, ethical approach to firing a person? and (2) Can the decision-making procedure be made more participatory? These exercises enabled the participants to gain some insight into the complexity of business decision-making and to have direct experience with role-playing as a pedagogical device.

The next session was devoted to planning. Having reflected upon Dr. Dolbeare's ideas regarding the structure of the Summer Institute, the group began to make its own decisions about how best to proceed. After some discussion, they agreed that there should also be some consideration of how the content being discussed could be effectively communicated to students in the classroom. With these parameters in mind, the group worked out a tentative schedule for the next few days. The most important consequence of the planning session was that from that day forward the participants assumed ownership of the Institute. It was now collectively their Institute, since they were responsible for determining its future direction.

Fr. Kirby arranged to hold the next meeting at the Jesuit house on Cazenovia Lake. This magnificent house provided a setting which encouraged informal conversation and the forging of friendships. The focus for discussion was *The Federalist Papers,* writings which scholars view as the decisive interpretive source for the U.S. Constitution. Anyone seeking to understand the meaning of justice in the context of democracy in the United States must examine the ideas proposed in this document. The group discussed the implications of selected passages from *The Federalist Papers* for an understanding of classical American liberalism. In addition, the group engaged in preliminary planning for a debate to be held at the beginning of the last week. The facilitators would divide the group into four debate teams. The focus would be the pastoral letter, *Economic Justice for All.* At the end of the day, a dinner provided an opportunity for all to relax and enjoy one another's company.

The next session continued the discussion of *The Federalist Papers.* Their major economic implications were examined to gain some insight into the nature of our economic system. Then, themes from Karl Marx's *Communist Manifesto* were juxtaposed with classical liberalism to shed light on the different conceptions of economic justice underlying both systems of thought. Joseph Schumpeter's classic treatment of capitalism in *Capitalism, Socialism, and Democracy* provoked a lively discussion of his claim that capitalism would gradually transform itself into socialism. Participants raised questions about the relationship between capitalism and democracy. If democracy means that people have control over their own lives, is it compatible with the structure of capitalism? What would it mean for the people to be in control of their own society? As participants reflected on these readings, some tentative conclusions began to emerge. First, to understand ourselves and our idea of economic justice, we must understand the social and historical setting out of which we have emerged. Second, our view of economic justice is at least partially contingent upon our social and historical context, and other contexts will produce different views. Third, there are different concepts of economic justice at work in the world today, leading to different perspectives on such issues as third-world debt. The difficulty in establishing a global perspective is rooted in our generally unreflective commitment to a certain way of viewing the world.

The facilitators next presented their plan for the debate on the pastoral letter. Participants were organized into four teams representing the following perspectives: liberation theology, classical free-market liberalism, Burkean conservatism, and modern populism (based upon *The Populist Moment* by Lawrence Goodwyn). The question for debate was: Shall the proposals of the pastoral letter become the public policy of the United States government? Sufficient time would be given for initial presentations, preparation of questions to be addressed by the other teams, response to questions, and an open discussion. The remainder of the session was devoted to a discussion of Goodwyn's treatment of the populist movement in the United States in the late nineteenth century. Participants considered the question of whether such grass-roots movements are possible in the United States today. This discussion marked the end of the group's treatment of historical sources and a transition to the issue of what to do about economic justice, given this insight into the history of the problem. The four debate teams met separately to plan for the next day's debate.

Week Three:
What should we do about economic justice?

For the debate on the pastoral letter, participants were grouped in such a way that practically no one had an opportunity to defend his or her favorite position. The participants enthusiastically argued for the positions they were assigned and, as a result, came to see the pedagogical value of such debates. To do well, one was forced to develop a sympathetic understanding of a position for which one had no previous sympathy. All four teams found ideas to support and to criticize in the bishops' pastoral letter. For example, the team representing liberation theology praised the bishops for their stress on the centrality of a preferential option for the poor. However, they criticized the bishops' failure to condemn capitalism as the cause of poverty in the world. Participants quickly realized that in order to carry out this exercise successfully, they had to achieve a firm grasp of both the theoretical foundations of their own perspectives and the content of the pastoral letter. The debate turned out to be a transforming experience because faculty saw themselves in the role of students and realized the pedagogical value of small-group activities.

Participants then spent some time reflecting on the debate. A major criticism was that each group tended to treat the pastoral letter selectively so as to advance the merits of its own perspective. As a result, the spirit and content of the pastoral letter were lost. Then, the attention of the participants turned to the matter of planning for the remaining days of the Institute. They introduced a number of themes for consideration. These included the relationship between the Jesuit tradition and the teaching of values, the meaning and implications of professionalism, and the purposes of values education and their relationship to the classroom. Participants agreed that the next day's topics would be (1) Fr. Langan's reflections on the history of the pastoral letter and (2) a group discussion of Paolo Freire's text, *The Pedagogy of the Oppressed.* Some time would also be reserved for setting the agenda for the last three days of the Institute.

Fr. Langan began the next session by giving insight into the philosophical and theological traditions out of which the pastoral letter grew. The bishops originally intended to write a letter on capitalism, but then decided to limit their focus to the economy of the United States. The letter serves to remind middle- and upper-class Catholics of their own origins and their obligation to the poor. Among its limitations are its hope that a harmonious synthesis among diverse and opposed economic interests can be achieved, and the fact that the document is the product of a committee which had to reconcile different points of view.

The participants then turned their attention to an examination of the different models of social change proposed by the U.S. bishops and Paolo Freire. After some discussion of the relationship between the economies of first- and third-world countries, participants spent the rest of the afternoon planning the activities of the last three days. The first topic for discussion would be the place of professionalism, ideology, and other cultural factors in contemporary society. Next, some time would be devoted to small-group brainstorming sessions on the nature of Jesuit education at Le Moyne College and the place of values in that educational tradition. The small groups would then report the results of their conversations; discussion of those results would follow. The last meeting would be devoted to a consideration of how the momentum established in the Institute could be carried forward after its conclusion.

Dr. Dolbeare distributed an outline which set the context for discussion. He suggested that individuals operate on four levels in their dealings with the world. The first and immediate level consists of our perception of 'reality' through the senses and our engagement in practical activities. The second level is that of ideology, understood as the way in which we interpret everyday experience in light of basic values and assumptions. The third level consists of these basic values and assumptions. The final level, the epistemological, represents our way of thinking about and recognizing 'truth.' Unless we become aware of our epistemological commitments, we cannot make free choices about level-three matters. Discussion of these levels led to a consideration of what function professionals serve in society. Do they (we) act to keep the lower classes in their place, or do they (we) hold society together? Towards the end of the session, the facilitators distributed the assignment for small-group activity. The topic was: What should values education at Le Moyne College consist of, what would the 'product' be, and how can teachers appropriately help shape that 'product?' Each individual had a copy of the college's statement of objectives, a short selection from the *Ratio Studiorum*, and a summary of a document entitled *The Characteristics of the Jesuit Tradition of Education.* These documents would become the focus for small-group discussions.

After the small groups spent an afternoon discussing these documents, they selected one member to give a summary of each group's ideas. These summaries were organized into four general categories: (1) what the group found to be of positive value in the vision of Jesuit education depicted in the readings; (2) what problems members had with this vision; (3) how the vision applied to Le Moyne; and (4) opportunities for change at Le Moyne. After the presentations, the participants considered what they as faculty members could do to achieve at least modest changes. They agreed that they could best utilize their energies by becoming part of the Values Group. They then divided into three subcommittees for a brainstorming session. The question considered was: How can we advance substantive knowledge regarding economic justice at Le Moyne College, improve teaching and the quality of student life outside the classroom, and change the institutional reward structure?

The last meeting of the Institute focused on ideas generated by the three subcommittees. With regard to advancing substantive knowledge, participants proposed such ideas as the development of an annotated bibliography on the topic, the establishment of a day for campus-wide discussion of economic justice, and a presentation as part of the freshman orientation program. In response to concerns about teaching and student life, they suggested such ideas as occasional meetings for sharing the results of teaching innovations and student-faculty seminars in the dormitories. Finally, they recognized the need to change rank and tenure procedures in order to reward effective teaching and service to the community. They then agreed to meet during the fall semester to share ideas and attempt to promote some incremental changes in the quality of life at Le Moyne College.

Now that we have examined the activities of the first Summer Institute, let us return to the issues of pedagogical method and content raised in the opening incident. Institute participants discovered that different methods of learning were effective devices for dealing with the content of economic justice and could be incorporated into their courses. They also realized that their reflections upon economic justice were not confined within the boundaries of an academic discipline. Rather, their own historical, social, and professional context provided the framework for discussion of content. The recognition of the connection between pedagogical method and content grew out of their understanding that methods of learning work best when the content is situated in a context relevant to the learner.

The Shortcomings and Strengths of the First Summer Institute

Any activity undertaken for the first time is bound to produce surprises. This section of the chapter will focus on an examination of the outcomes of the first Summer Institute. At the outset, it is important to note that in the eyes of most participants the Institute was a resounding success. The energy generated over those three weeks helped sustain a variety of positive changes, both in and out of the classroom, during the 1988-89 academic year. Both participants and facilitators had an opportunity to evaluate the Institute. The following remarks are based upon their comments.

One evident shortcoming had to do with planning. For a number of reasons, it proved impossible to bring two of the facilitators and the participants together prior to the start of the Institute. The advance planning done by the facilitators was tentative. Enthusiasm began to grow once the participants assumed ownership of the Institute—once it became *their* Institute. The only way to establish ownership from the outset is to have everyone involved in the planning process from the beginning. Our learning of this lesson contributed to the success of the second Summer Institute.

A second shortcoming involved scheduling. The ideal schedule would be a Monday, Tuesday, Thursday, Friday pattern of meetings for three weeks. This pattern would provide a break in the middle of each week for participants to prepare for what was to come next. The limited availability of the facilitators forced the adoption of a more compact schedule. As a result, participants had little preparation time, a fact which limited what could be accomplished. We learned that facilitators should be selected based, in part, on their ability to meet an established schedule. But this option is not always workable (as we learned during the 1989 Institute), given limited advance notice for planning the Institute. Obtaining commitments from outside facilitators at least one year in advance would go far in solving these first two shortcomings.

The final shortcoming was perhaps not really a problem at all. The Values Group hoped that a significant portion of the work of the Institute would be devoted to the preparation of new course modules incorporating issues of economic justice into the existing courses taught by the participants. This did not happen in the first Summer Institute. The participants discussed how the theme of economic justice could be introduced into courses, but the actual planning for course changes did not take place for two reasons. First, the participants themselves made the final decisions on what the Institute schedule would include. They were content to undertake course modifications individually after the conclusion of the Institute. Second, before course modifications of the sort hoped for could be undertaken, some more fundamental issues related to the nature of one's professional life at Le Moyne College had to be carefully addressed. Three elements became the major concerns of the participants: (1) planning, (2) investigation of source material related to economic justice, and (3) self-examination in a social and historical context. This left hardly any time for what might be called nuts-and-bolts planning.

On the positive side, the Summer Institute provided an opportunity for serious interdisciplinary discussion of a common issue. As the discussion unfolded, it became apparent that no single discipline, not even economics, had a privileged position of insight into the many dimensions of economic justice. The participants had to pool their intellectual and personal resources to advance the inquiry. The fact that a group of academics representing different disciplines could pool resources in such a congenial manner is itself remarkable. One of the facilitators, reflecting upon his experience with the group, commented:

> You produced an excellent group of faculty participants, well diversified by field and by level and character of interest in developing new approaches. Everybody was open-minded, all did their readings as far as I could tell, and at least six or seven were genuinely creative—which has to be far beyond the usual expected average. The "mix" was good also, in that practically everybody was willing to expose their serious thoughts to the others, and practically everybody was really willing to listen to their colleagues as if they had something to say.

The aims of the Institute were mainly cognitive in nature. What we did not anticipate were the affective changes that would occur as a result of the growth of a sense of community. One of the qualities of contemporary American life is its excessive individualism. As products of that culture, faculty members can easily become isolated from one another by focusing on their own research interests. The Institute opened up new avenues of communication which have enriched the ongoing life of the college. Perhaps the most important long-term consequence of a series of Summer Institutes will be the sense of solidarity among the faculty. We are aware that engaging in an experience like that provided by the Summer Institute is an effective first step in the direction of building a genuine community. We now understand that our aim must be to extend this sense of community, not only to students and staff, but also to the larger communities of which we are all a part.

How has the Summer Institute enabled faculty to stimulate student thinking about economic justice? First, the participants have experienced directly a variety of pedagogical techniques—role-playing, small-group activity, simulation exercises—and so will return to the classroom prepared to use some of these techniques. Second, they are now convinced that economic justice is not simply an issue for economists and ethicists. Rather, it has profound interdisciplinary and human implications. Third, they have undergone the transforming effect that active engagement with a topic creates and, thus, they see the intrinsic connection between pedagogy and content. Finally, they have formed a community which can be called upon for support as they undertake experiments in the classroom.

Endnotes

1. Cf. Lawrence Kohlberg, "Moral Stages and Moralization: The Cognitive-Developmental Approach," in Thomas Lecrona, ed., *Moral Development and Behavior* (New York: Holt, Rinehart and Winston, 1976), pp. 32 ff.

2. Cf. Carol Gilligan, *In a Different Voice* (Cambridge, Mass.: Harvard University Press), pp. 18 ff.

3

The 1989 Summer Institute

A Roman Catholic bishop, a Reinhold Niebuhr Professor of Social Ethics, a well-known American historian, an associate academic dean, and a group of Le Moyne faculty members—some with long careers and some in their first year of teaching—are blindfolded, working in pairs attempting to mold identifiable objects from messy wet clay. No one knows the identity of his or her co-sculptor. Touching hands provide the only means of communication. Who are these people and what are they doing? These busy, albeit for the moment silent, workers, are participants in the second Le Moyne Summer Values Institute centered on the theme of peace and war.

This exercise in cooperative clay modeling was but one event in a three-week Institute; nevertheless, it represents in many ways what is distinctive about the Le Moyne Summer Institute. Like the Le Moyne Values Program of which it is a part, the Summer Institute takes a multifaceted approach to values education and seeks not simply to instruct faculty but also to engender in them the willingness to deal with values issues in and out of the classroom.

Created by the Values Group to have an impact on students through the faculty, the Institutes attempted to model an approach to education in which the participants themselves are responsible for the development of the topic. To do this, faculty members had to be empowered to raise values questions as part of the curriculum as well as to respond to student-initiated discussions. Few faculty members busily engaged in research and the pursuit of their own disciplines have the luxury of devoting substantial periods of time to digging deeply into the issues of other disciplines. Faculty members find it difficult to keep up to date on the best intellectual thought about current social issues unless they are part of their own disciplines. This occurs not from ill will or lack of concern about these issues, but as the result of the normal human need to deal with the more pressing matters at hand—the next class, the next committee meeting, or the next article.

Summer Institutes are designed to meet faculty needs in dealing with values questions in two basic ways which can be referred to by the shorthand phrase: "content and process." "Content" deals with the intellectual aspects of a topic. "Process" is less easily defined because it is broader than the how-to of incorporating values into a syllabus. It includes considerations of classroom management, such as whether a teacher stands or sits, how grades are assigned, or how students are addressed. But it is not just an exchange of teaching tips, such as how to get a silent student to participate. Process is all this and more. It involves something of a transformation in the way members of the Summer Institute approach not only values issues but their students, indeed their very relationships to each other and the larger community. In addition, given the multidisciplinary nature of both the faculty involved and the facilitators, participants have an opportunity to appreciate the contributions other disciplines can make to the solution or understanding of modern social questions. In this context, facilitators—even a bishop and distinguished scholars from other universities—become not simply lecturers imparting knowledge but sharers in an exploration into how to assist students in dealing with the values-laden issues of modern society. And so it was that the bishop and the other scholar-teachers were blindfolded, silently messing in clay in an exercise to demonstrate the necessity for trust and cooperation if peace is to be realized.

Learning from the First Institute

The 1989 Summer Institute on peace and war built upon the experiences of and was related to the first Institute on economic justice in 1988. Even though the bishops' pastoral letter, *The Challenge of Peace,* had been written prior to the pastoral, *Economic Justice for All,* the Values Group decided to treat the issue of economic justice first as a foundation for understanding the impact of military expenditures on social programs. The first Summer Institute, however, taught the Values Group more than content and process. Out of it emerged a new understanding of the strengths and weaknesses of operating a summer institute.

In order to understand the dynamic in the Institute's process, the director for the second Institute attended several days of the first Institute, met with some of the participants shortly after its close, and watched the videotapes of the closing sessions. In addition, the evaluators' report, based upon questionnaires completed at the close of the first Institute, provided valuable insights. Four significant considerations emerged for the planning of the second Institute: community building, the critical role of the local Le Moyne participants, the need for clear goals and purposes, and the fatigue factor.

First, community building was an unexpected but highly desirable result of the first Institute. Given the time to engage in extended theory-practice conversation, many faculty members had learned for the first time the nature and scope of their colleagues' teaching or research efforts. New friendships as well as new research alliances had been formed. The participants had grown in respect for one another and achieved a new appreciation of the quality of the Le Moyne faculty.

Second, the faculty participants themselves had provided much of the richness of the learning experience. It had become clear that although facilitators from outside the college were important in legitimizing the Institute, the Le Moyne participants shared the burden of helping one another learn. Because the faculty participants had been selected to represent many different disciplines, their individual expertise complemented and expanded that of the facilitators. Each participant could be expected to draw upon his or her discipline to bring new insights or approaches to a values issue.

Third, the Fellows had come to the first Institute with sets of expectations which sometimes were at odds with those of others. The evaluations indicated that some participants had wanted more information about how to incorporate values issues into their courses, while others hoped to spend significant amounts of time digging deeply into textual criticism. Still others desired extensive exploration of creative teaching methods. It had taken valuable time during the first Institute to attempt to resolve these different expectations, and although some needs had been met, others had remained unsatisfied.

Finally, the videotapes as well as the anecdotal reports of those attending the first Institute clearly disclosed that three weeks of intense intellectual work had been physically demanding. Pacing the second Institute would be important. There had to be time for additional reading, planning for presentations, and absorption of the experiences.

Selecting the Facilitators

Not only did we now have a more realistic understanding of the Institute's strengths and weaknesses, but we also knew that certain qualities were needed in facilitators and that it was critical to convey to them a precise sense of the Le Moyne Institute. To foster a sense of community, facilitators clearly *had* to have qualities beyond that of being experts in their fields. If the faculty participants were to develop their own strengths as a significant source of knowledge within the group, the facilitators *needed* to be able to share their understanding of the topic and yet not dominate the discussions. They *had* to be willing to participate as group members while acting as outside commentators who could summarize a discussion or indicate new directions to be explored. To meet the participants' pedagogical needs, facilitators *had* to be selected not only on the basis of their intellectual credentials, but on their abilities as teachers and as participants in group discussion and activity. They would model effective teaching through action as much as words. The qualities required of the facilitator sounded like the Le Moyne guidelines for full professor: a creative person who is a superb scholar-researcher, superb teacher, and superb in relating to students and colleagues.

The committee for the second Institute, composed of the directors of the first and second institutes and the director of the Values Program, worked more than five months on the selection process. Many people were asked for suggestions, phone calls were made, and schedules were checked and rechecked. Finally, the team of Dr. Roger Shinn from Union Theological Seminary in New York City; Dr. David O'Brien from Holy Cross College, Worcester, Massachusetts, Auxiliary Bishop Thomas Costello from the Roman Catholic Diocese of Syracuse, and Dr. Barron Boyd from Le Moyne College was assembled.

These facilitators had expertise in various areas of the topic. Bishop Thomas Costello is an educator who for many years directed the diocesan school system. Also he had participated with the other American Catholic bishops in formulating and voting on the pastoral letter, *The Challenge of Peace*. He was able to discuss not only the content of the letter, but also the process by which the bishops had arrived at the text which was finally disseminated. In the context of the Values Program, the collegial and consultative process followed by the bishops provided an example of how a group can work together to articulate commonly held values. He shared with the group his own reactions to the various drafts of the letter to help the participants understand the nuances of language the bishops used. Because of his work in preparing himself for voting on the various drafts and amendments to the letter, he was a valuable resource for many aspects of the issue of peace and war.

Roger Shinn is an international scholar and consultant to governmental and church agencies. The author of numerous works on peace and war, he had been a soldier and a prisoner of war during World War II, and was willing to share his experiences. Because of his long teaching career, he was able to remind the group of important events or writings relevant to the discussion. He often remained quiet during discussions, then offered insightful summaries which laid foundations for further exploration of issues.

David O'Brien was selected in part for his work as an historian with expertise in the history of American Catholicism, and his position as current chair of Peace Studies at Holy Cross College. In addition, as a professor in another Jesuit college with some experience in the recent drafting of that school's mission statement, he was not unfamiliar with the Jesuit tradition of Le Moyne College. His experience was helpful in discussions on the role of values education in the college curriculum. In addition, he had connections with the pacifist movement in the United States which enabled him to provide information and literature reflective of this movement. He also recommended several relevant films which were valuable additions to the resource room that was set up to allow participants to share books, articles, and other materials that related to the general topic.

The planners of the second Institute also took the first step to make future Institutes more in-house: they chose a facilitator familiar with the Le Moyne faculty, who could draw upon their intellectual strengths and monitor their physical energies. Barron Boyd from the Political Science Department was selected as a respected faculty member who had also been a Fellow in the first Institute. With a specialty in international politics and South Africa, he would bring his own perspective and depth of understanding to the Institute's topic. Once selected, Barron Boyd joined the planning committee to make final preparations.

Formulating the Agenda

The first event of the Summer Institute occurred on an icy day in March when the Le Moyne participants and outside facilitators met for a day-long planning session—a critical new component of the second Institute. The first Institute had been initially planned by the director and the facilitators. Planning the agenda for the second would involve all the participants from the very beginning.

This planning meeting posed two simple questions for participants: what do you expect to get from the Institute? and how might your goals and the goals of others be reached? The responses to these questions allowed everyone to hear the expectations of the Fellows; it also signaled the beginning of the participatory process which has become a hallmark of the Institutes. This planning meeting was important for two reasons: it not only began forming the group into a community, but it also established the group's responsibility for the process and progress of the Institute. The Institute was not to be the sole responsibility of the facilitators. The planning session itself modeled a learning experience in which students (here the faculty participants) helped shape the curriculum. The initial agenda could then be better formed to meet the needs and to utilize the abilities of the participants. By hearing the various expectations of other participants, each member would have a more realistic understanding of the multiple needs the Institute would attempt to address.

One outcome of this initial planning meeting was the decision to deal with the topic of peace and war from a variety of perspectives: realism, idealism, environmentalism, liberation theology, and feminism. The participants suggested combining an exploration of pedagogical techniques with the various perspectives by assigning each participant a topic area and asking each to present his or her perspective in an interesting or innovative way. This was an important step in the blending of the Values Group's concern for content and process.

After the larger planning session, the facilitators and the director met to discuss a tentative agenda. Although there was an overall plan for the three weeks, it was subject to daily adjustments as the group's needs and interests evolved. From those suggested at the planning meeting the facilitators selected five books which reflected the multidisciplinary nature of the Institute. These included the bishops' pastoral letter, *The Challenge of Peace: God's Promise and Our Response,* because it had been the inspiration for the Institute's theme. Two novels were chosen, *Ridley Walker* by Russell Hoban and *All Quiet on the Western Front* by Erich Maria Remarque (the latter because it was one of two books that incoming freshmen were to read in preparation for orientation week discussions on peace and war). Roland H. Bainton's *Christian Attitudes Toward War and Peace: A Historical Survey and Critical Re-evaluation* and Jonathan Schell's *The Fate of the Earth* completed the list. The director arranged to have the books available to the participants by early May so that they could be read before the beginning of the Institute.

The facilitators planned to meet the participants' time and energy needs by scheduling Wednesdays as a day off from the otherwise grueling pace of meeting from nine in the morning to three-thirty or four in the afternoon. On the other days, the facilitators tried to vary the pace by interspersing more difficult discussions with less demanding material. The director made sure that drinks and snacks were always available in the meeting room to replenish flagging energies. Lunch provided in the faculty dining room refreshed both body and spirit. On Fridays, a sandwich lunch was served in the meeting room. These Friday lunches provided an unexpected opportunity to extend the morning's discussion or to watch an additional film or video. Nevertheless, for many the first week's routine was distinctly tiring.

Learning the Topic

Many things happened during the Institute. Rather than providing a comprehensive listing, I will instead recount a few moments and incidents in each week to provide a flavor of the events. A recommendation made at the planning meeting was that the Institute begin with a screening of the film *Dr. Strangelove.* This proved to be an extremely valuable means of getting the discussion started because all the members of the group began on the basis of a shared experience.

Indeed, watching movies became an important part of the Institute. Although scheduled as a day off, one Wednesday was devoted to watching several films recommended by various members of the group. The films were viewed not only for what they could contribute to understanding the issues of peace and war, but also for their potential as catalysts for classroom discussion. The films indicate the range of exploration and suggest the issues being addressed. *Atomic Cafe,* a humorous approach to the problem of atomic weaponry, strings together film clips and cuts from television shows of the fifties and early sixties. While many enjoyed this look at the past, most thought the film too dated for use with students. The World War II documentary, *Assault on San Pietro,* was a difficult film for one of the facilitators who had fought and been captured in that war. Following the film, he shared some of these personal experiences with the group. *Two Women,* involving the experiences of a woman and her daughter in Italy during World War II, was such a moving experience for the watchers that the often jocular comments that were common during the watching of films disappeared. When the film ended, no one wanted to add commentary on the impact of war. The final film of the day—*Rambo II*—was included so that participants might experience students' exposure to war as depicted in modern "action" films.

The first week's discussions dealt primarily with the bishops' pastoral, *The Challenge of Peace.* Bishop Costello explained the terminology of the pastoral and the process of revision and compromise which produced the final document. One afternoon Roger Shinn described "just war" theory, the process by which it had developed, and how it related to the principles in the pastoral. Among other things, he described how wars which may start out on an apparently just basis seem inexorably to be drawn into less than just tactics. For example, in World War II it was the Allies' policy not to bomb civilian areas. This policy changed, however, as the war escalated. The Allies justified the bombing of civilian areas by claiming that they had become part of the military complex.

That afternoon, one of the faculty members who had just finished her first year of teaching at Le Moyne suggested that Thucydides' "Melian Dialogue" from the *Peloponnesian War* was appropriate to the discussion of just war theory. Although a tentative schedule had been prepared by the facilitators, it gave way to incorporate a discussion of this debate between the Athenians and the Melians. The director arranged for distribution of the text, and the faculty member led the discussion on the following day.

On Thursday afternoon, Barron Boyd set the stage for a war room simulation. Each participant was assigned a role, such as member of the President's staff, the Cabinet, or the Armed Services. Barron played the role of President in order to control the process. The issue was whether the United States should bomb a factory in another country believed to be producing poison gas. Some members arrived on Friday morning dressed for their roles; all were prepared intellectually to take on their respective tasks. Following the simulation, the facilitators pointed out that no one specifically raised just war theory during the exercise even though it had been prominent in discussions during the week. Nevertheless, the participants believed that the theory's arguments figured in the simulated war room decision-making processes and acted as limitations on actions that might have been recommended.

During the second week, one day was devoted to the question of whether faculty members should be incorporating values concerns in their syllabi. It was clear to the Values Group that, given a faculty which is both religiously and politically diverse, this issue had to be addressed with sensitivity during the Institute. An address on the role of Jesuit education given by Fr. Peter-Hans Kolvenbach, S.J., superior general of the Jesuit Order, was used as the catalyst for the discussion of raising values issues in the classroom. To underscore the importance of the discussion as well as provide a comfortable atmosphere for the exchange of ideas, the members of the Institute met at the Jesuit Villa House on a nearby lake. In spite of, or perhaps because of, a steady downpour, the discussions were long and fruitful, although they did not produce agreement on all points. Dinner and abundant snacks kept the discussions congenial.

Because the first week had been largely devoted to a discussion of issues related to war and weapons, the last two weeks focused more on peace issues by exploring the obstacles to peace from a variety of perspectives. In order to devote a full day to each perspective within the time frame of the Institute, the facilitators had selected four areas: realism, idealism, environmentalism, and liberation theology.

When the four topics were announced, the Fellows immediately expressed concern that no group would deal with the feminist perspectives which had been discussed at some length at the planning meeting. Because the Institute, as part of the Values Program, is envisaged as a participatory experience, the participants' concerns were taken into consideration and a fifth

group was formed by realigning the members, adding the director as a participant to keep each group to a minimum of three
people, and reducing the time devoted to each of the topics. The
members of the original and the realigned groups were selected
not on the basis of expertise, but on the basis of interest in learning about a new area, although some effort was made to include
at least one person in each group with some expertise in the
area.

To accommodate the desires of the Fellows to deal with
pedagogical issues while also addressing content areas, each
group was given a double task. First, group members had to
help participants understand the obstacles to peace from the
group's assigned perspective, either those caused by the group's
focus or those that inhibit the group's participation in peace efforts. Second, the group had to do this in an innovative
pedagogical way.

A set of introductory readings for each of the topic areas had
been compiled by Barron Boyd, the facilitator from Le Moyne,
from suggestions made by the participants and the facilitators.
The readings had been distributed prior to the Institute and
enabled all participants to become familiar with at least some
basic concepts in each area and provided a starting point for each
group's presentation. During the second week, the afternoon of
the first day and the morning of the second day were designated
as study times, creating an opportunity for each group to research its area and plan its presentation. The facilitators were
available in the college library as resource people to assist the
groups.

The end of the second week and the beginning of the third
were devoted to the five presentations. Although it had been
planned that each group would have a full day, the addition of
the fifth topic meant that each was allotted a half-day session,
with several groups getting slightly more time. When the assignment was given, it seemed a painfully short period in which
to deal with an entire area. Nevertheless, the groups managed
to present their ideas effectively. Because sessions ran approximately two-and-a-half to three hours with a mid-session
break, the time available for presentations more closely ap-
proximated the normal classroom period of fifty to seventy-five

minutes. This gave Fellows a better opportunity to experiment with what can be done in a class setting.

Each group worked diligently on both the content and the process aspects of their assignment. A few examples will disclose some of the richness of the experience. Because inability to trust was identified as one of the obstacles to peace from the idealists' perspective, the clay exercise described at the beginning of this chapter was one method used by the group to demonstrate the building of trust. The clay modeling was followed by a discussion of the experience. The participants described how they had felt about being blindfolded, what methods had been used to communicate, and whether they had felt part of a cooperative venture or controlled by the other person. It is worth noting that this exercise has since been used effectively by one of the Fellows at a workshop at which she wanted to establish graphically at the outset that the persons attending had the ability to work together on the difficult issues in an atmosphere of trust.

The realists showed an edited version of the play, *A Walk in the Woods*, in which a Russian and an American arms negotiator attempt to deal with the negotiating process by informal, friendly discussions away from the bargaining table. To prepare for the discussion of whether war is inevitable, the Fellows had been asked to read short selections from several authors, including: Thomas Hobbes, "On the Natural Condition of Mankind"; Hans J. Morgenthau, "Politics Among Nations"; and Charles Kegley and Eugene Witkoph, "Idealism and Realism in Foreign Policy."

The realist group adapted the social scientist's game commonly known as "The Prisoner's Dilemma" and called it "Guns or Butter." The game involved international cooperation to reduce the level of arms expenditure, resulting in increased goods and services for the citizens of the respective countries. Some players were more cooperative than others and benefited their citizenry while maintaining military arms at a similar level to that of their opposition. This game demonstrates several valuable aspects of the Institute. First, not only do the Fellows of a given Institute help each other, but there is also an enhanced level of colleagueship among all the Fellows from all the Institutes. In this case, the basic information about the game had been provided by a Fellow from the first Institute to assist a Fellow from the second in preparing her presentation. Second, the Institute provides an opportunity to try new techniques and experiment with new material. The Fellow who developed "Guns or Butter" had never run a simulation before, and had the opportunity to test it and herself on her colleagues rather than making a first attempt in a classroom. Following the game, the participants suggested ways in which the game could be made more realistic and present the issues more clearly.

The environmentalists argued for an ecology of peace, a world which balances diversity and functional interdependence. A biologist in the group described species which occupy biological niches, thereby avoiding conflict with other species. For example, studies have indicated that five species of wood warblers occupy different but predictable areas in the branches of a tree. An historian in the group presented the response of Chief Seattle to an offer by President Franklin Pierce to buy land occupied by the Native Americans of Puget Sound. To stimulate discussion she asked four questions: What are the characteristics of Chief Seattle's relationship to nature? In what way does it contrast with that of the white settlers? How do you think the cultures came to generate their particular relationship to nature? How can a relationship with nature function as a barrier to peace?

The group presenting the perspective of liberation theology dressed as campesinos and held a press conference to provide their views. So that participants could experience deprivation, they had arranged with the director to withhold the morning coffee and doughnuts at least for a time. Following the press conference, the participants were asked to imagine themselves as campesinos and describe what they would like to see happen in their lives in the next ten years. The responses were examined to determine whether the desire for education, advancement, and freedom from fear of reprisal could be achieved in a peaceful way, or whether confrontation was inevitable. The film, *The Mission,* was shown to stimulate discussion.

The feminist group made the final presentation and seized the opportunity to incorporate and in some measure synthesize the prior discussions. To set the stage for discussion, the participants were asked to read an article describing the varieties of feminist thought. The group began their session using story-telling as a means of providing personal experiences of conflict or peace-making and to set the tone for group sharing. To make the connections between the feminist approaches and the other topic areas, each group (the realists, the idealists, the environmentalists, and the liberation theologians) was asked to reconvene and reconsider its approaches to issues of peace and war in light of feminist values and then to report on their impact.

Because of the intensity of the reading and discussion, Friday afternoons were often reserved for more relaxed pursuits. One was devoted to an exploration of various poems, including an exegesis of "Nineteen-Hundred-Nineteen" by an English professor who is a recognized Yeats scholar. For many in the group it had been some time since they had devoted any concentrated attention to this type of analysis. This activity provided one of the many opportunities for participants to be learners again and to grow in respect for their colleagues.

Understanding the Program

The final two days of the Institute focused on how to translate the experiences of the Institute into classroom and extracurricular activity, how to assist students in addressing values issues from a multidisciplinary perspective. To do this we first described the concept behind the Values Program at Le Moyne, its decentralized structure and grass-roots nature. Then we discussed the role participants could play in the process. As the day progressed the group arrived at an image that described the Values Program at Le Moyne: the hub of a wheel with many spokes. At the center of the wheel is the faculty and student concern for values questions. Supporting this concern are the spokes, such as the Summer Institutes and Academic Forums. The Values Group that sponsored the Institute understood that the infusion of values concerns into curricular and co-curricular activity is important. The Summer Institutes are spokes because they prepare faculty for participation in the process. The Academic Forum expands coverage into co-curricular activities by presenting different perspectives on a values issue throughout the year. The evaluation process assists in the planning for the Institutes and explores the impact of the program on student values. Other essential spokes are the soliciting of funds as well as the seeking of support from the college administration and staff. Disseminating information about the program is necessary to insure participation and understanding by the Le Moyne community and to share its experiences with other colleges and universities. Institute members were encouraged to become active members of the Values Group and contribute their energy to the efforts necessary to insure that the spokes support the hub.

One spoke, that relating specifically to students, is very important. During the previous year a Student Values Committee had been formed within the Student Senate Academic Affairs Committee to complement the Values Group and insure that programmed activities would meet the needs and interests of students. The chairpersons for the Student Values Committee attended meetings of the Values Group and acted as liaisons between the two organizations. One of the student chairpersons was hired by the Student Life Office for the summer to create a process for dialogues between students and faculty members on the issues raised by the Values Program. At one of the final sessions of the Institute, the student presented his plan and sought the faculty's help as presenters, discussants, or simply as participants at meetings or dinners. He came armed with sign-up sheets so that enthusiastic faculty could be enlisted on the spot. These faculty members would be a resource for the resident hall advisors who are required to facilitate at least one discussion each semester. Virtually all of the participants agreed to serve in some capacity.

Planning for the Classroom

For the final day, the Institute's participants focused on values concerns and the curriculum. The faculty members were asked to describe how material on peace and war could be incorporated into their syllabi or how the Institute would change the way they approached teaching. Most faculty members readily agreed that values questions can be dealt with in religious studies or philosophy courses, but one goal of the Institute is to legitimize values concerns across the curriculum. Everyone seemed willing to try new material or new teaching approaches. Some wanted to make changes or additions to their syllabi; for others the very way in which they approached teaching had been altered by the experience of the Institute. A few examples will indicate the creative ways Fellows planned to deal with peace and war in a variety of disciplines or to incorporate new, more value-conscious teaching methods.

A business department faculty member specializing in management information systems believed that she would incorporate values issues into her case-oriented course, "Decision Support Systems." One of the cases she uses deals with the decisions made by a particular company. During the Institute she had viewed a tape of a trial involving the company which raised questions about the company's involvement in weapons production. She planned to have the students discuss the case, then show the film, and ask if the students' view of the company's decision-making process was altered by this additional information. Because managing information involves decision making, she also wanted to incorporate material on conflict resolution.

A professor of mathematics wanted to incorporate classroom techniques which made better use of the students' abilities to assist in course development. He planned to develop his class materials to provide more opportunities for all students to participate in discussion. Student suggestions for his required reading list as well as student annotations would be solicited. In addition, he wanted to use some exercises to build trust among his students, especially in the pre-med math courses.

A political scientist thought that she could induce students to discuss values issues by asking them to respond to various questions related to peace and war by stationing themselves along a numbered spectrum. Each group would then discuss and explain its position. Students could move to a different location if they either changed their position or felt that another group more closely described their understanding of the problem.

A sociologist, who was a member of the group that presented the liberation theological perspective, thought it would be a good idea to develop some mini-courses on peace and war topics, such as a course on terrorism. During the Institute, one of the Fellows had shared a videotape her daughter made of a conversation with one of the hostages held in Iran. The video had prompted a discussion of terrorism, its causes, and its consequences. Although the sociologist had been considering dropping the course on "Conflict Resolution," he now resolved to keep it in the catalog. In addition, he planned to use *Hiroshima* as one of the texts in his "Death and Dying" course.

A member of the religious studies department wanted to try teaching in a non-hierarchical fashion. She proposed starting the class with no syllabus except for a series of readings drawn from a wide variety of sources and relevant topics. The syllabus would be developed by the students through discussion of the readings.

A professor from the English department specializing in Irish poetry saw many ways to incorporate peace and war into his syllabus. He planned to use some of the feminist perspectives in his course on Romanticism, to be more sensitive to the competing issues in his handling of the Irish troubles, and to incorporate some discussion of the internalization of physical violence. He appreciated the experience of being a student again, and resolved, to be more empathetic to his students' trials.

Many people were convinced that the use of film was an important way to draw students into a discussion and to legitimize the raising of ethical issues. One faculty member, who usually had students undertake an oral book report, decided to add a one-on-one discussion of a movie to his course requirements.

Problems to be Resolved

There surely are a number of successes to report from the Summer Institutes. They have probably succeeded beyond the expectations of the group that initially conceived them, but no account can be complete without a recognition of some of the problems that still need to be solved or frustrations that have not yet been overcome.

As the account of the last day of the Institute shows, the Fellows have expressed high resolve to change their courses and their teaching approaches. Some will make changes, others will not. To date there has been no requirement that Fellows must document changes in their syllabi as a condition of attending the Institute. In planning for the first Institute, the Values Group decided that it was more important to use its limited financial resources to allow more faculty members to attend the Summer Institute, and trust their good will in following up, rather than to reduce the number of participants and use the extra money for stipends for course revisions.

In many respects this decision reflects the nonauthoritarian, decentralized, grass-roots approach characteristic of the Values Program. This is due in part to the belief that getting faculty members to discuss values questions in the classroom regardless of the topic, and to recognize the values choices implicit in their methods of teaching remains more important than incorporating material relevant to any specific values issues. This approach represents a valuing of values—an agreed belief that the most important goal of the Values Program is to have questions of values raised on the Le Moyne campus. The topic selected for a Summer Institute thus becomes a vehicle for achieving that goal rather than an insistence upon specific course content.

The planning committee for the second Summer Institute believed it important to include faculty, administrators, and students as participants in the Institute to better reflect the makeup of the Le Moyne community. Including administrative people was relatively easy. Administrators work throughout the summer and therefore did not need an additional stipend. All administrative heads had no difficulty in allowing a staff member the time necessary to attend the Institute. Nominations were solicited from the administrators and the Values Group. Two persons were selected, although one withdrew just prior to the start of the Institute.

The associate academic dean was an important participant because she is responsible for the Freshmen Advisement Program and works with the Freshmen Orientation Committee. She already had some contact with the Values Program because discussions of issues related to the 1988 theme, economic justice, had been incorporated into both freshmen programs. Incoming freshmen had been sent two short readings to prepare for the discussion. The venture was successful. For the second year incoming freshmen were asked to read two books, *All Quiet on the Western Front* and *Hiroshima,* and to prepare answers to specific questions for the discussions. In addition, the involvement of the associate academic dean in the Values Program and the Institute has been an important means of obtaining administrative support. Through her efforts, the academic vice-president and dean now incorporates support for the program within his budget.

Including students has proved to be a major hurdle. While there are students eager to attend, monetary and philosophical considerations present the chief obstacles. The problems are many. Should students be compensated for attending the Institute? If so, how much? Can they be given tuition reduction in lieu of cash payments? Is the presence of one or two students of benefit to the whole student body or only to those selected to attend? Would students be intimidated among so many faculty members? Would the faculty be hesitant to discuss certain issues if students were present? Because the last question was raised as a most serious objection by participants already selected, the director of the second Institute scuttled the plan to include students. She and others felt that the participants' expectations, based on the first Institute, should not be changed after they had submitted their applications and been selected.

At the end of the Institute, the Fellows proposed many plans for continued activity during the next year. Ongoing discussions, the creation of a file cabinet of relevant materials, work on team-taught courses, more sessions on pedagogy, and faculty colloquia were but a few of the suggestions. Promises were made to bring the group together and to pursue these ideas. While many people have pursued individual ideas, the participants have only met as a group for a holiday social gathering.

Undoubtedly there are many reasons why follow up has not been effective, but two seem to stand out. The first was the failure of the program to plan for follow up. No one was explicitly given the task of continuing the process, perhaps because the focus of the program is basically on students. While Fellows were encouraged to participate in the Values Program by attending planning meetings or participating in Academic Forum activities, no formal process had been developed for continuing the discussions begun in the Institute. The second reason relates to time and energy. At the end of the Institute, everyone was tired. There was no energy to formulate a plan for the fall. Everyone wanted and needed a rest. By the time school reconvened in the fall, the enthusiasm of the Institute had receded and been supplanted by other concerns related to the Values Program or other aspects of being an academic.

The final concern about the Institutes is the problem of funding. Fund-raising is difficult and time consuming. It has cost between forty and fifty thousand dollars to run each of the first two Institutes. One of the group's major tasks is to find a way to continue the Institutes when that level of funding cannot be found.

The bright side is that the Values Program has developed a process for providing the college's faculty and administrators with a unique experience that does more than allow for intellectual learning about values and ways of dealing with values questions in the classroom. The Summer Institutes offer a faculty member or an administrator the experience of dealing with values issues in practical and intellectual ways. The community-building aspects ensure that there is a support group to assist in expanding a participant's interest. Faculty members and administrators are empowered not only to discuss a particular Summer Institute topic, but the topics of later Institutes as well.

4

The Academic Forum

Introduction

Students flow into and out of a college teacher's life. Two, three, possibly four years is all the time we have to make a positive impact. Our efforts are further circumscribed by other factors beyond our immediate control. Much of a teacher's success depends upon the academic quality and personal characteristics of the students themselves. And much also turns on the educational atmosphere, the expectations and opportunities of the institution. We cannot do all we would like. It is thus gratifying, instructive, and a bit unsettling when we encounter students who overcome the deficiencies of their school, who create their own atmosphere, expectations, opportunities and, hence, learning experiences.

Eleven years ago I encounted just such a group of students. Average in most respects, drawn from various majors (Political Science, Biology, Philosophy, Economics, History, Industrial Relations, Psychology), not knowing one another beforehand, these nine men and three women gravitated together in their freshman year. Like other students their age, they were interested in dating, partying, and getting by. But as a group they developed concerns about their intellectual and personal growth. For instance, most were involved in extracurricular activities (community service activities, the college newspaper, student governance). Their grades were significantly above the norm (six graduated *cum laude*, three *magna cum laude,* and all went on to advanced degrees). They had late evening parties that were sometimes transformed into discussions of current events, personal ethics, social policy, and the like. They took advantage of the college's established opportunities and developed new options (clubs, trips) when Le Moyne came up short. They consciously constructed a supportive environment which encouraged each of them to take ideas and values seriously, to think and talk intelligently, and to act ethically. These particular students learned outside as well as inside the classroom, and that learning resonated in their academic careers, personal lives, and community activities. Their success, achieved in spite of the shortcomings of our institution, poses the challenge the Values Program faces: to find ways of encouraging and supplementing the process of self-education so that the majority of our students follow the learning model this group represents.

Origins of the Academic Forum

In its first year, the Values Group spent much of its time discussing reforms that could respond to this challenge. We quickly eliminated wholesale restructuring of the curriculum because Le Moyne had just gone through an unsettling core curriculum revision. Suggestions to continue that process would have been futile. Indeed, we rejected all proposals to modify the curriculum—setting up new majors, requiring experiential coursework, proposing a new values-based course. These attempts, we concluded, would threaten certain college constituencies, involve many difficult implementation problems, or promise only limited impact. Instead, we settled on the idea of a faculty development program directed at modifying existing courses and improving teaching skills appropriate to values education. This concept eventually grew into the Summer Institute. However, the Values Group felt that programs affecting the students outside the classroom also had to be included as part of the overall plan. Thus, our original vision included the recognition that "student development" must accompany faculty development.

In its initial year, the Values Group deliberated over a number of ideas for improving extracurricular education. None was rejected. Rather, each was subsumed as a potential proposal within the larger effort to shape the extracurricular environment of the college. We agreed on a title with sufficient ambiguity and flexibility to allow for an array of values-enhancing activities. The "Academic Forum" would be a series of learning experiences throughout the academic year designed to introduce values education into all aspects of student life. By offering a program of out-of-class activities focusing on the theme of that year's Summer Institute, the Forum would complement, integrate, and reinforce the values-laden issues and ethical concepts raised and developed in the classroom. It would follow the "interactive model," the theoretical basis for the entire Values Program.

Key to the success of the Academic Forum in this model was the variety of interdisciplinary events falling under the Forum umbrella: keynote addresses, lectures, debates, panels, faculty colloquia and workshops, first-year student orientation and advisory meetings, workshop-retreats for student leaders, films, trips, student art and essay contests, poetry readings, student-faculty dinner-discussions, library exhibits and art shows, musical and theatrical performances, liturgical celebrations, and "teach-ins." This diversity of formats was to parallel the diversity of departments and populations targeted by these different events: business-related majors, science majors, socially aware and involved students, active campus leaders, students in the humanities and social sciences, commuting and part-time students, the immediate college neighborhood, the larger Central New York community, alumni—somehow, all would be touched and transformed. Just as faculty from all disciplines were invited to the first Summer Institute, students from all majors were viewed as potential constituents and beneficiaries of the Academic Forum. In effect, this campus-wide immersion in the Forum's theme represented a curricular innovation designed to break down the barriers between classroom and out-of-classroom education, between faculty and students, between different disciplines, between acquiring information and refining one's values.

How the Idea Developed

Conceived to promote extracurricular education, the idea of an Academic Forum matured under the influence of three main developmental forces: one pedagogical, one thematic, and one institutional. First, the Forum evolved from the Values Group's educational purposes. Second, it reflected our concern with economic justice, the focus of the first Summer Institute. And third, it was shaped by the liberal arts mission and religious traditions of Le Moyne College.

Pedagogical objectives date to the very origin of the Academic Forum. As previously mentioned, the Values Group sought to create and test an alternative technique for educational reform. Historically, most teaching innovations have focused on changing faculty-to-student interaction. Faculty attempt to adjust their courses to make them more values-oriented, student-centered, or content-relevant. This, of course, is precisely the thrust of the Summer Institute. New course proposals, team teaching, field research, debate formats, or similar standard approaches promise to change the classroom environment.

But these top-down reforms are necessarily limited. Education, values oriented or not, is predominately an extracurricular experience. Merely compare the time spent in class to that spent in the dorm, the library, the dining hall, the recreation center, and other out-of-classroom venues. If higher education cannot reach students there, in the artificially constructed "real world" of most residential campuses, then their unreinforced classroom experiences will have minimal impact. The point is that education, especially values education, must also be attended to after the schoolbell rings.

This analysis raises two basic questions. How can the faculty and administrators at an institution such as Le Moyne make the out-of-classroom experience more educational? And how can a college's or university's students, faculty, and administrators be integrated into a socially conscious learning community?

The Academic Forum was developed as a means of addressing these questions. Among those wanting to improve the educational experience outside the classroom was Le Moyne's Residential Life Office. The college's residence halls normally house 60-65%

of the full-time students. Supervisory personnel have been professionalized in recent years, with most now possessing a master's degree. Their increasing concern about the intellectual quality of campus life, a concern not exclusively Le Moyne's, found a ready response in the concept of the Academic Forum. Ideally, through this program student-faculty interaction would flourish, and club activities would be more focused, cohesive, and popular. The notion of a collective learning community would take root and grow. And further, these developments would counteract the "warehousing" image of dorm life, always repudiated in theory but often accepted in practice.

If all this could be done, a different student would enter the class. Many on the faculty would have already acquired new approaches and materials on the issue of economic justice and on values education generally through their participation in the Summer Institute. Now able to take advantage of the intellectually enriched and ethically sensitized campus environment, these teachers would find in their classrooms more participative educational co-workers: students immersed, as a result of a variety of programs, in the values-laden issues of the year's theme. Faculty development changes only one-half of the learning equation. The Academic Forum is designed to affect the other half, to provide the college with a supportive program of student development, thereby giving faculty and students a common framework and a shared enthusiasm.

A second force shaping the idea of the Academic Forum included both the theme of economic justice, the topic chosen for the first Summer Institute, and the Values Group's catalyzing reading, *Habits of the Heart*. The moral tension within the American psyche between individualism and community, between personal freedom and social obligation, between self-interest and a concern for the common good, a tension poignantly illustrated in Robert Bellah's book, speaks directly to the issue of economic justice. We intended through the choice of this theme to put in stark relief the overarching question posed by *Habits of the Heart:* Can we simultaneously seek public virtue and private success?

The original Values Group and the participants from the first Institute grappled with this basic cultural and ethical dilemma.

We wanted our students and colleagues to grapple with it, too! But there would be resistance. Our society encourages a narrowness of perspective: what is significant for me is what affects me directly, materially, individually. Both this narrow definition of self-interest and the consequently instrumental nature of our relationship with the larger community are fostered by a political system that handles conflicts regarding inequality (economic, racial, gender) as if they are disputes merely requiring group accommodations. Negotiations substitute for moral discourse. The bargaining process allows all parties to maintain separate identities, reinforces those separate identities, and defines collective problems in terms of private cost-benefit calculations. Inequality is simply not perceived as a social problem and, therefore, it is not perceived as a values issue, a justice issue, a moral issue.

This analysis explains the sources of the resistance we expected when we asked students and faculty to think about economic justice. The language of the "public interest" is not used in these discussions; the language of political conflict dominates. Because the process of bargaining does not promote personal moral reflection, it can achieve no moral consensus. And thus, instead of lessening our sense of alienation, societal problems such as inequality pose a threat from which we seek refuge in our separate insularities. Worse still, the parochial perspective we see within our society is even more apparent and appalling when we try to relate as a nation to other cultures and governments in addressing international problems.

In its initial conception, the Academic Forum was designed to weaken this sense of individual isolation by encouraging a social sense of self. Events would promote empathy within the audience, an identification with the ideas and feelings of those in distress. As we consciously and deliberately expanded our notion of self-interest, we also would expand the awareness of private success to incorporate a personal theory of community, public virtue, and economic justice.

One event stands out as a successful example of this process of change. Starting the second semester of the Academic Forum, on January 23, 1989, the Human Services Association, a student club composed primarily of natural science majors, sponsored a traditionally structured event on poverty in Central New York.

A panel of experts reporting on health, nutrition, and housing problems faced by the regional poor was transformed by the unplanned involvement of welfare recipients in the audience. Even the sympathetic panelists could not cope with the frustration, anger, and fear expressed by these victims of the welfare bureaucracy. This exchange of views and emotions was not lost on those in attendance. No dry academic exercise, the event brought to breathing, standing, screaming life the problems of the often-invisible "other America." How can we pose issues of economic justice so that they truly touch the individual? The experience of that panel supplied one answer: challenge the insularity of the individual, force the "self" to understand the "other." Put another way, the challenge to the Academic Forum was to develop opportunities for students and teachers to confront the reality of economic deprivation and injustice.

The third factor influencing the development of the Academic Forum is the religious background of Le Moyne College. Many of the expectations associated with the Forum grew out of Le Moyne's Jesuit and Catholic tradition, especially its emphasis on values-based education and social service. Among the stated purposes of a Le Moyne education is guiding students to "dedicate themselves to lives of informed service to others." This goal is not unique to Le Moyne; most colleges and universities acknowledge their liberal arts heritage by displaying similar statements in their catalogs. But the social service ideal gains added substance and support at this college from the religious values upon which it was founded. A desire to educate the whole person ("knowledge joined to virtue"), a special concern for the interests of the poor ("preferential option"), active involvement in helping the community ("the faith that does justice")—these principles of Jesuit and Catholic education define Le Moyne's mission, demarcating the common ground upon which our culturally, religiously and ideologically heterogeneous faculty can meet and work. These public statements of our institution's values provide both the legitimizing context and the compelling reason for the Values Program.

The Academic Forum connects the traditions of this school to the actions of its students, before and after graduation. By calling into question the specialized, fragmented, compartmentalized conceptions of the "self," the entire Values Program seeks to promote a pro-active student (and faculty and administrative) response to economic injustice, one that goes beyond "what" and "why" to "why not" and "how." Education ought to be an agent of change. Analyses of present conditions ought to include both value judgments and the behaviors those judgments generate. The Jesuit tradition hopes that values-based learning provides the student with factual knowledge, social awareness, moral commitment, professional skills, and personal confidence—in sum, empowerment.

Let me stress this point since it relates not only to the Academic Forum but also to the Values Program generally. Students are frequently viewed as passive mental receptacles, and teaching as a transfer of information, a process of filling up the mind with "facts." In this tradition of value-free objective inquiry, what is learned and how it is taught should be devoid of values. The Values Group and Le Moyne College as a whole do not operate from this tradition; we do not accept its assumptions. Furthermore, we deplore its consequences—academic detachment and passivity. It is because we expect and demand more from education that personal and social values are important. They are the bridge between knowledge and action.

Constructing that bridge is a central goal of the Values Program. Among the outcomes we seek is enabling students to recognize that they can make a difference regarding the problems and issues discussed in and out of class. Equally important is encouraging a realization that they ought to make a difference, to actualize their values in career decisions, personal relationships, and social involvement. We want to engender a sense of "values efficacy," not in terms of some weekend project that promises instant success or, more probably, instant frustration and cynicism, but rather in terms of a lifelong commitment to the resolution of significant human problems.

We knew early on about this program's potential for indoctrination, that in heightening awareness and developing skills we would also be fostering a particular brand of commitment, a particular agenda for social action, a particular set of values. This was clearly not in keeping with our sense of responsibility as educators or our interpretation of the program. But while we were sensitive to the issue of indoctrination, we also wanted to push students to develop their own morally defensible position. "I'm OK, you're OK," is not OK! "Values awareness," as such, is not our ultimate purpose.

Forum events often presented different and conflicting ideological orientations—ideological pluralism is a check on indoctrination. However, diversity does not legitimize every point of view, and therefore the Forum's tolerance was tempered by the purposes for which the Values Program was created, the problems it sought to resolve. Institutional tolerance and academic freedom would not become covers for moral bankruptcy. Events and presenters had to support some conception of economic justice and social responsibility along with the reasonable expectation that people act on that conception of the common good. The Academic Forum was designed to discourage the narrow economic concerns and the pervasive personal alienation which impoverish moral discourse and hamper political participation.

First envisioned as a complement to the work of the Summer Institute, the Academic Forum soon developed its own structure when the Values Group sought to put the program into effect. Pedagogy, theme, and institutional tradition were the guiding forces for the faculty. However, as with so many other campus projects, the Forum had different purposes for different segments of the college community. Students and administrators who became involved in planning and implementing Forum activities saw the program as a vehicle for student participation and organization, or as an arena for raising emotional policy issues. Their views, too, were reflected in how the Forum actually worked.

Organizing the Academic Forum

The Academic Forum's operating structure that first year is best described as "decentralized" and "ad hoc." We were forced to rely on this type of structure, but soon recognized its ironic contribution to our success. The Values Group's grants financed the Summer Institute and research components of the overall program, but the Forum had to depend on internal monies. Making a virtue out of a necessity, the Academic Forum director (selected by the Values Group), key students in student government, and administrators in the Residence Life Office created an informal network to exchange information, plan strategy, and coordinate events. The network lacked not only official imprimatur but also self-recognition as a group. However, the term "network" indicates the informal organizational relationship and decision-making process of that first year.

Everyone understood the need for motivation, for getting people invested in the process. Student clubs, academic departments, and administrative offices had to volunteer to develop and sponsor their own activities focused on their own constituencies. Without money to "buy" student involvement in a faculty-directed, centrally coordinated program, the network had to "sell" the concept of a values-based Academic Forum devoted to economic justice to every potential activity-sponsoring group (club, department, office).

The irony is that the lack of external money and the fragmented patterns of funding at Le Moyne forced the Values Group to adopt a procedure for the Academic Forum appropriate to the essence of the Values Program. There was doubt whether a top-down approach could have generated broad-based student involvement, even with outside financial resources. Fiscal exigencies, however, offered us no choice. We developed a bottom-up strategy. Consequently, the network was a resource, sometimes a catalyst, but very rarely the sole agent for an event. Here was a student-centered program that required grass-roots student leadership and support for its success. This meant student willingness to create, organize, publicize, fund, and, of course, attend events. The Academic Forum thus became a concrete example of student empowerment.

A brief chronology of the beginning months of the Academic Forum would best explain the operating structure that evolved. A keynote address given in April of 1988 by Dr. Richard Morrill, one of the facilitators in the first Summer Institute, initiated the public phase of the Values Program. The speech and the attendant publicity generated student and faculty awareness of the general program and built momentum for the following fall semester. The Academic Affairs Committee of Le Moyne's Student Senate became the focal point of student interest, and the Values Group stayed in contact with the committee's leaders. But despite promises of cooperation, everyone remained uncertain of exactly what to expect.

The Residence Life staff increasingly came to see how the co-curricular activities of the Academic Forum could be incorporated into its own program. In the summer of 1988, incoming freshmen were sent two highly readable articles addressing the theme of economic justice ("The Ones Who Walked Away from Omelas," a short story by Ursula Le Guin, and an excerpt from *Narrative of the Life of Frederick Douglass, an American Slave*). These pieces became the springboard for small-group discussions during Freshmen Orientation Week. Facilitators for the discussion groups were recruited from Summer Institute faculty and from students who had expressed prior interest in the Values Program. This turned out to be the Forum's first successful event, utilizing the informal network that would oversee the development of the Academic Forum for the remainder of the academic year.

The Residence Life staff decided to get involved with the Values Program in part because it thought the Forum might become an effective vehicle for achieving its own objectives: a more diverse, educational, cohesive, and interesting array of out-of-classroom experiences. This reasoning proved to be a model for building broader support within the college community. To paraphrase and reverse John F. Kennedy: ask not what you can do for the Academic Forum, ask what the Forum can do for you. This is not a flippant answer to the problem of how to get various campus constituencies to attend, coordinate, and especially initiate events. Getting students to invest in a program that had not yet been institutionalized in any meaningful way was and remains difficult. The process we happened upon, based on shared responsibility and control, open communication, and mutual interest, seems to work.

We did receive some institutional backing. In September, a letter from the college president to all prospective sponsors (student, faculty, administrative and staff groups) officially announced the year's theme, economic justice, and requested that each group undertake at least one activity in accordance with the theme. Follow-up letters from both the Academic Forum director and student leaders reiterated the invitation to participate, promised consideration of any idea and support for viable projects, and indicated whom to contact. When outside funding was still a possibility, the Values Group had hoped to organize monthly subthemes for the Forum. November 1988, for example, would focus on the United States and the Third World, while events for March 1989 would address women, children, and economic justice. However, this plan was dropped as the decentralized nature of scheduling events became evident and inevitable.

Sparked by the three letters mentioned above, several individuals approached key members of the network to suggest event ideas in various stages of development. A student brainstorming session added other possibilities. When a member of the network or a particular professor or a determined group of students followed through on an idea, it was then placed on a master calendar. With different events having different lead-times, and some activities dependent upon the availability of a specific faculty member, student, administrator, or outside participant, there was little chance of fully coordinating this creative chaos, except perhaps for preventing events from overlapping. The calendar also contained events not developed for the Academic Forum but in harmony with its theme. For example, Women's History Week included a lecture by Raquel Rivera on "Voices of Hispanic Women." Any activity that had a clear values element dealing with an aspect of the theme was fair game for Forum support. In addition to the usual publicity for individual campus events, a separate Values Group flyer listed the Forum events for the coming months. The network utilized other ways of spreading the word: ads in the school newspaper, a targeted city-wide mailing (on events appealing to the broader community), and the Syracuse media (when coverage was likely). The college community knew something was going on; the network was not shy about getting its message out. However, to avoid any charges that the Academic Forum was taking over the event, the club or department sponsors—that is, those who paid the bills—were always featured in the advertising.

The scheduling process and, in fact, the entire organizational structure of the Academic Forum were highly decentralized, pluralistic, and ad hoc. The Forum depended upon voluntary participation that was not centrally controlled, administratively coerced, or financially induced, and it succeeded, because of its very structure, to reach in some fashion a majority of students and faculty.

Putting on the Show

The Academic Forum was not exclusively academic. If we were to achieve the various objectives originally set for the program, we would have to produce a show, to entertain, and to motivate an audience. Any attempt at student programming must take into account the problem of campus apathy. Though advertising, free food, and professorial pressure can increase the size of the crowd, what will insure that people stay and truly listen? The traditional format for college events is part of the problem of campus apathy. It entails an expert talking at non-experts with the obligatory question-and-answer period at the end. But it does not work as frequently as people think. And if we often failed to attract the numbers we had hoped, that failure can in part be attributed to this format.

Perhaps numbers should not be the chief criterion of an event's success. Different events reflect the interests of different groups on campus, and each must have its own voice and its own platform. But we ought not ignore the fact that the platform is part of the values-imbued message. Students do not respond to a "show" that treats them as passive observers. They attend but do not learn. On the other hand, interactive programming causes a ripple effect, creating opportunities and incentives for more learning and the personal behavior-shifts which effective education generates. After such events, further ideas and actions evolve, and the synergy of personal and social change is likely to continue. We tried to keep faith with the Values Program's assumptions. That is, the process of the event itself—the way it is staged, the way information and ideas are presented, the way different types of participants interact—

would reinforce the overarching message: comprehension, compassion, and commitment.

Some events clearly did not fit the typical pattern of expert speaker and passive listeners. In addition to the activities known as South Africa-Le Moyne (see chapter 7), other programs were designed to be more interactive, participatory, and student-centered. After a student play about worker alienation and class differences in England (*Slab Boys*), the audience and theater people (stagehands, director, actors) exchanged views about its meaning and relevance. For the freshman advising program, six professors performed a short role-play exercise on bank investment decisions and moderated a student discussion on public obligations and private business policy. Students who had visited and worked in an impoverished region of Mexico during summer break showed slides of their trip, talked about their individual experiences and collective feelings, and then asked audience members for their own reactions. Students have a sense of what will work with their peers, and we (administrators and faculty) should give space and trust to their creativity and judgment.

One event that illustrates the utility of the interactive learning model enlisted the cooperation of three Summer Institute participants and two classes of students. The departments of Religious Studies, Political Science and Sociology sponsored *Poletown Lives*, a documentary about the conflicts arising from an urban economic redevelopment project in an ethnic Detroit neighborhood. Students in two courses, "Urban Politics" and "Corporate Responsibility," developed a project that integrated the film with their coursework. After previewing *Poletown Lives* and reading extensive background materials on the Poletown case, the classes sought to find points of common ground among the protagonists (Detroit officials, neighborhood residents, and General Motors representatives). Following a well-attended public showing of the film, students reported on their conclusions and led the audience in a discussion. The faculty did little more than set up the assignment. This exercise demonstrated to all involved that students benefit more from creating and presenting an event integrated into their classwork than from attending an event disconnected from their campus life.

Another activity, occurring in April of 1989, became a capstone event for the year's Academic Forum. Billed as a "Town Meeting on Economic Justice" and sponsored by the college's Office of Continuing Education, the event focused on drawing the larger community into the campus dialogue on economic justice. The town meeting idea meant that somehow the audience must become part of the activity. The method chosen by the main organizer was both devious and simple: showmanship would supplement scholarship.

A professor of Philosophy who had participated in the 1988 Summer Institute decided to construct a ruse that would encourage the "town's citizens" to participate. Two speakers were introduced and proceeded to lecture on the problems of poverty. After each had sketched his own point of view, this mock debate was interrupted by vociferous objections from the floor: a woman on welfare complaining about raising her children in the ghetto, a factory worker recounting how his family worked its way up the economic ladder, a professional woman afraid about taxes going up, a Marxist radical criticizing capitalism. Spaced around the auditorium, these well-rehearsed student actors gave flesh and blood to the economic theories the previous two speakers had espoused, and they added an emotional energy so often lacking in academic debates. The audience soon recognized these stereotypes as part of a larger "show," but the shock-value of their performance remained. A panel of "real" experts then addressed the issues of economic justice in light of the ideas and feelings of these "real" people. Finally, the moderator asked faculty (some of whom had been prompted ahead of time in case the conversation flagged), students, and community people to continue the discussion.

One idea that did not initially achieve its potential was that of faculty-student discussion groups. Summer Institute participants were to lead a series of informal seminars in which students could explore the issues raised by Academic Forum events. Attendance would be voluntary, but student leaders and Residence Life staff assured the Values Program that student involvement would be strong. Additional inducements included a modest stipend for the faculty and a dinner—not the typical cafeteria gruel—for the students. These social-academic happenings seemed to be a wonderful way to break down student-faculty and dorm-classroom barriers.

Though interest was high, only one discussion group on economic justice met that first year, and its success proved to be no precedent. The reason was clear. With our decentralized approach, good ideas fell through the organizational cracks. The Values Group's attention was directed at other project components, its human resources stretched to the limit. Unfortunately, despite genuine enthusiasm, no students, faculty, or administrative personnel had chosen to take this program under their wing. We continue to have faith in the idea, and we will still incorporate some version of student-faculty discussion groups in future grant proposals. But we await an organizational structure that would guarantee that someone takes responsibility for implementing this part of the Values Program.

This chapter should also note outcomes of the Academic Forum that were more long-term or intangible. A list of activities does not indicate the changes in campus atmosphere brought about by the existence and visibility of the overall program. As a specific example, the original Values Group discussed including a social service component. How better to connect the academic work of students to the social needs of the community? How better to underscore the importance of living one's values in an informed and responsible way? However, since many Le Moyne students already engage in volunteer community work, the group decided to exclude this idea from its grant proposals. Nevertheless, the idea did not disappear. The Values Program had become not only a source of innovation but also a resource for others to use in introducing their own proposals, a mechanism for legitimizing nontraditional values-oriented projects. For example, an adjunct professor wanted to explore the possibility of a service learning center at Le Moyne; the current locus for the development of this idea is the Values Group.

Perhaps the most significant contribution made by the Academic Forum and the Values Program is in generating creative energy and providing the organizational space that energy needs in order to create. Enhanced expectations have encouraged faculty to experiment with new courses and new teaching approaches, students to form new groups on campus offering different extracurricular activities, and administrators to heighten Le Moyne's public profile and renew its public purpose. The cumulative effects of these changes have improved the learning atmosphere here at Le Moyne.

Conclusion

Modern higher education cannot keep pace with the career expectations of its consumers. It cannot because it offers a product fundamentally different from individual financial success. Students cramming for a test on Chaucer, or manufacturing a term paper (the third that week) on Hobbes, will ask "so what?" "why care?" and "what difference does this make?" Colleges and universities lie when they try to answer these questions and justify their missions in terms of careerism. They are perpetrating a fraud, and we all know it. Our goal is not training but education, not transmitting objective information but developing judgment. And though a good education might be reflected in a student's career choice, work satisfaction, and job performance, its worth is not and should not be determined by the marketplace. We should spend some time thinking about what education means.

Recall the group of students I discussed in the beginning of this chapter. Their individual concerns regarding choosing majors, keeping up averages, examining job options, and formulating career strategies did not obstruct their collective learning. They undertook the task of education. I want to think that Le Moyne College contributed substantially to their success at that task, but I suspect otherwise. Creating an environment within which such learning is not exceptional or coincidental, but is in fact a planned and anticipated consequence of our institutional structure—this is the ultimate goal of the Values Program generally and the Academic Forum specifically. It is a challenging and achievable goal worthy of our greatest efforts.

Part Two:
Personal Reflections

5

A Sociologist's
Perspective

Introduction

As I write, it is about eleven years since I finished my Ph.D. During the period since that time, my teaching and research have focused on the impact of public policy on American families. At Le Moyne, I teach courses such as "Marriage and the Family," "Law and Social Science," "Urban Sociology," "Work-Family Relations" and "Introductory Sociology." Before coming to Le Moyne, I also taught graduate courses at Wayne State University and the University of Rochester in "Public Policy Analysis," "Evaluation Research Methodology," and "The Family and Public Policy." Most of my recent writing has dealt with two issues: (1) family structure among the expanding American urban underclass, and (2) the impact of attorneys who represent low-income children in abuse/neglect proceedings.

Given this set of interests, I came to the 1988 Summer Institute on economic justice with substantial enthusiasm. When I reflect upon the origins of this enthusiasm, I can locate at least two sources. First, I should note that I joined the Le Moyne faculty in the academic year (1987-88) preceding the Summer Institute. I had spent my first year at Le Moyne occupied with preparing several new courses and chairing the Department of Sociology. Hence, while I had met and worked with many members of the Le Moyne faculty previous to the Institute, I still considered myself very much a novice to the institution and its faculty. Given this, I viewed the Summer Institute as an opportunity to come to know more of my colleagues and to lessen the degree of caution that I had exercised in meeting with them during my first year.

Second, I have dealt with the issue of economic justice in my research and writing on low-income families for over a decade. Most of this work, however, is highly specialized. It is addressed mainly to other social scientists and to state and federal agencies. Further, not a small part of it was produced in the framework of what is commonly referred to as "contract research." Finally, for better or worse, most of this work was produced under the "publish or perish" pressure at the institution with which I was affiliated before coming to Le Moyne. I stand by the integrity of the work I have published; however, I also believe that some of my work, at least in part due to the circumstances outlined above, has become too specialized, and perhaps less socially valuable, as a result. Technical professional journals have a preference for technical professional writing. What all of this means is that I came to the Summer Institute eager, perhaps even longing, to hear what my new colleagues— historians, economists, literary scholars, mathematicians, accountants, biologists—had to say on the issue of economic justice.

What I have reflected upon thus far addresses to some degree the questions of who I was and what I expected of the Institute when it began. Turning next to the experience of the Institute itself, there are two major areas in which I have found its impact to be substantial, perhaps even profound. These impacts can be delineated under the categories of networks and pedagogical models.

Networks

The network of colleagues with whom I work at Le Moyne was significantly enhanced because of my Summer Institute experience. In this respect, it is important to recognize that Institute activities included not only traditional academic work such as reading and seminar discussions of reading, but also exercises such as role playing, debates, and small-group projects. In these small-group activities the membership of the groups constantly shifted. Because several of the projects involved late afternoon and early morning preparation sessions, each small group typically had the opportunity to work intensively for more than a short period of time. What this format fostered was the development of intellectually and ethically demanding working relationships with colleagues with whom I would not normally have had the opportunity to work.

In retrospect, what strikes me most about the work in these exercises is that it gave rise to rather high levels of mutual *respect* and *trust*. It might seem odd that respect and trust should be singled out as notable impacts of a faculty development program at a small Jesuit college. However, Le Moyne traditionally prides itself on an academic environment that is informal, cooperative, and indeed, family-like. As a social scientist who has worked at several other quite different academic institutions, I feel confident in asserting that Le Moyne possesses such characteristics to a much greater degree than other institutions, particularly larger institutions. Yet it is also the case that Le Moyne is bureaucratically organized and that interests, particularly professional interests, tend to be differentiated along the lines of specialization built into the various administrative units. Practically, this means that opportunities for Le Moyne faculty to work on substantive intellectual and ethical issues, such as economic justice, are not so much scarce as they are crowded out by other issues. These other issues, for example research and publication in one's field and curricular reform in one's department, while important, all seem to have a *competitive* aspect which puts limits on the development of interdepartmental respect and trust.

Because of the Institute's group exercises on the substantive issue of economic justice I had the opportunity to work with a biologist who specialized in ecology, a mathematician who teaches statistics to social science students, and an economist who, like me, studies the family and public policy. The list could go on, but the point is that through the Institute I *discovered* the Le Moyne faculty, or at least the nearly twenty percent of it that participated in the Institute, and I *trust* and *respect* most of them. Note, I am not saying that I distrusted or lacked respect for my colleagues prior to the Institute; rather I am saying that I had lacked the opportunity to develop authentic trust and respect. In some ways the Institute allowed me to step beyond departmental and bureaucratic modes of collegial interaction and to be empowered by a new set of human resources that I had known existed, but that I had not previously tapped. And, we had the opportunity to work relatively unfettered by the competitive aspects of the academic environment. My guess is that I would have discovered many, but not all, of these colleagues and their strengths eventually, but the Institute accelerated this process and focused it in a manner that has benefited not only me, but also my students. Before turning to pedagogical impacts of the Institute, a major class of the benefits to students, I want to provide a few illustrations of network-related benefits of the Summer Institute.

I love to run and I love to talk, and I found a colleague at the Summer Institute who enjoys these activities as much as I do. Bill Miller, a mathematician, and I had known each other only slightly before the Summer Institute; we had worked on one committee previously. (See chapter 6.) At the very outset of the Institute, we discovered that we both enjoyed a noon run and so throughout the Institute we ran at noon and talked about the progress of the Institute and its impact on us. Since the Institute, the running and the talking have continued. It is the talking and the effects of the talking that I see as a major impact of the Institute. Research on teaching in higher education strongly suggests that teaching strategies are discipline-specific and that relatively little in the way of interdisciplinary pedagogical exchanges actually occurs. Research also suggests however, that when these exchanges do occur, they are extremely valuable.[1] Bill and I constantly talk teaching. We talk about our efforts at innovation in teaching; we talk about our successes; we talk out our failures; we each reformulate what the other says from the perspective of our own disciplines and we feed it back, often with the result that new insights are gained. We talk about projects with which we are involved, specifically those related to the Values Program. We talk about research we are conducting and papers we are writing. We talk about mathematical chaos theory and its applications to the modeling of social behavior. We talk about natural science and mathematics and the history and sociology of natural science and mathematics. We talk about the life of our college and how to improve it. We talk about our families. We talk about popular misconceptions about our disciplines. We talk about home repair. Perhaps these running/talking sessions would have started eventually under different circumstances, but the Summer Institute certainly has contributed much to the tone and the spirit of our running sessions. The sessions continue to enrich my teaching and the contributions that I believe I can make in other arenas such as the ongoing Values Program, counseling students, and college committee work.

Another discovery that I made during the Summer Institute was that there were several other members of the faculty who had substantive interests similar to my own—namely the family, the economy, and public policy—that dovetailed with the Institute's theme of economic justice. Two economists, Darius Conger and David Rogers, study gender, labor market dynamics, and family demography. Mary Collins, chair of the Department of Education, works in the area of family, children, and educational policy. Since the Institute, I have kept up contact with these colleagues and friends. Indeed, with this network as a core, I have been able to identify at least five other members of the Le Moyne faculty with interests in family, children, and public policy. This is a very large number of people with similar interests for a college faculty whose total number hovers around 120, and it represents a substantial resource for the community. Indeed, with the support of this group it was decided that the 1990 Summer Institute and Academic Forum would focus on families, children, and public policy. As with my "running/talking sessions" with Bill, the origin of the 1990 Institute may be found in the Institute of 1988.

Pedagogy

As I understood it, one of the major goals of the Summer Institute was to facilitate reflection upon pedagogy—specifically pedagogy related to ethical issues—among the Institute participants and to foster pedagogical innovation along those lines. To be honest, I've always been rather doubtful about the efficacy of what goes by the name of innovative teaching practices. For me, group projects, debates, small-group discussions, role playing, etc., were all weak substitutes for the finely crafted lecture in which students were encouraged to ask questions as the lecture progressed and the professor spiced the lecture with provocative questions placed at strategic points of transition in the analysis.

Needless to say, the latter method was my method or what I imagined my method to be and, after a decade of teaching, I felt quite comfortable with it. Not immodestly I would note that my student and peer evaluations always supported the notion that I did a pretty good job with this method of teaching. In behaviorist terms, the reinforcement that I have received for my teaching style has been very positive—which is to say that this style, so well learned, was not to be easily unlearned. And yet, to a much greater degree than I had expected, my teaching style was modified by the Institute. I have not abandoned my favored style, but I have altered it to include strategies, or variations upon strategies, used in the Summer Institute, strategies about which I was uncomfortable prior to the Institute. What I want to do next is to reflect upon certain aspects of the Institute that fostered these modifications in my teaching style, and then I want to provide some illustrations of the modifications themselves.

We did a great deal of role playing during the Institute. On the first or second day of the Institute, we were each given a case study dealing with a bank's decision about whether to close a branch office in an economically disrupted neighborhood. Next, we were divided into five or six groups, each representing parties with interests in this decision (e.g., the State Banking Board, the town mayor, the bank's central management, union representatives, representatives of the bank's stockholders, the bank's branch management, citizen groups, etc.) and given a half hour to prepare for a public hearing before the State Banking Board in which the closing of the branch office was to be considered vis à vis the bank's state-mandated fiduciary responsibilities. The public meeting lasted for about forty-five minutes, and we debriefed for another half hour.

In another exercise, we were each placed in one of four groups who were to debate the American Catholic bishops' pastoral letter on the economy, *Economic Justice for All*. The four groups were to argue from one of the following positions: liberation theology, American Populism (we had all read and discussed the historian Larry Goodwyn's *The Populist Moment*), Burkean conservatism, and free market liberalism. Each group was given its identity midway through the afternoon of the day before the debate. The groups went into planning and preparation sessions that afternoon, some met and worked that evening, and some came in early the next day to do further preparation. The debate was to take up a full morning.

The final exercise that comes to mind, although there were several others, involved the facilitators providing us with various contemporary documents that articulate, or seek to articulate, the educational mission of the Jesuit Order, excerpts from the Constitution of the Jesuit Order written by St. Ignatius of Loyola, and the mission statement of Le Moyne College as it appears in the college catalog. Again, we were broken into four or five groups. Each group was given the task of articulating the essence of the Jesuit tradition of education in relation to the issue of economic justice. As with the debate, the groups had an afternoon, an evening, and the early part of a morning to prepare for their discussions.

This is probably not the place to discuss in any detail the actual content and outcomes of these and other exercises that took place during the Institute. Suffice to say that the exercises were very powerful and creative experiences that to some degree changed one as a teacher and a person. What were some of the crucial characteristics of the Institute that fostered such transforming experiences?

First, it seems to me that we were especially fortunate to have as one of our facilitators Kenneth Dolbeare, a political scientist/lawyer who has dedicated much of his career to exploring and implementing innovative strategies for teaching social, political, and economic analysis. In his structuring of exercises and in his disposition and approach to all aspects of the Institute (e.g., discussion of readings, group decision-making processes, etc.), Ken provided a role model of "the teacher" that many of us found quite appealing, even if his model was not our own. I am a rather cautious person in general and, as I prepared to introduce modifications in my own teaching, I found it incredibly supportive to have someone as a role model whom I considered to be very successful at what he did.

Second, we worked damn hard preparing for each exercise. I recall spending hours analyzing materials on the Institute's demanding reading list, reviewing old books in my office (for example, books on the theology of liberation that I had not opened in ten years), working late into the night on presentations for the next day's exercise, and working in time-constrained small-group sessions in preparation for debates, forums, and role playing. The intense work involved in preparing these exercises dispelled my initial caution and suspicion that group and role-playing exercises were just a way of getting out of real work and wasting class time. I have come to believe firmly that if these exercises are done well, they involve as much or more work on the parts of teacher and student as do more traditional pedagogical styles.

I noted earlier that the Institute had engendered for me, and I suspect for others, high levels of *trust* and *respect* and that these sentiments formed the bases for the new collegial networks and sense of community that came to life as a result of the Institute. More than any other component of the Institute, the group exercises gave rise to this trust and respect. The exercises gave participants from very different disciplines a common ground of hard intellectual and ethical work that had a product, the group presentation—a product that most often made us very proud.

Third, if you think about it, most pedagogical innovations are conceived by teachers and *tried out* on students. We think that we have a good idea, and we give it a go. We experiment with an idea, an approach. Implicit, of course, in this developmental process is the fact that we play the role of experimenter while our students play the role of subjects. The Institute was effective for me as a teacher precisely because it took me out of the role of teacher and into the role of student. I was doing the exercises, not running them, and I believe that because of this type of work

I gained a more comprehensive sense of what will and will not work in group exercises, and why. I think that I have also gained a much deeper respect for students as a result of having become one myself and, I would add, I believe that I typically have had a much deeper respect for students than they have for themselves. What the Summer Institute did was to make the faculty, as a faculty, students again. In doing so it neutralized, to some degree, our dominant identities as disciplinary professionals. My sense is that this alteration of roles, if not identity, is a necessary condition for noncoercive pedagogical innovation.

Illustrations

To conclude, I want to present a series of illustrations of the sorts of adaptations, some small, some large, that I have made in my teaching and that I believe are attributable to the Summer Institute.

The first type of adaptation might be classified as new materials that have been integrated with my courses. The Institute's reading list was formidable. Further, many Institute fellows brought materials of their own devising for us to share. These sorts of materials have found their way into most of my courses. For the sake of brevity and because the exposure that most Le Moyne students get to sociology comes through our introductory course, I will use SOC 101, "Introduction to Sociology," to illustrate how Institute materials have become a part of my courses.

The tragedy of the commons

I introduce students to the sociological theory of institutions with Garrett Hardin's famous story of the tragedy of the commons. The story is about a group of herdspeople, a commons with a fixed grazing capacity, and the conditions under which the uncontrolled pursuit of individual profit on the commons leads to its destruction. The story is well known to ecologists and social systems analysts. I use the story to introduce the notion that human existence is inextricably interdependent in nature and that human institutions (the family, the state, markets, religion) represent efforts to respond to the tragedy of the commons when the specific conditions giving rise to it occur. I try to drive home to students the proposition that the underlying problem the tragedy of the commons illustrates is very real and that institutional solutions vary greatly in terms of how "just" they are. Dictatorial states can regulate the commons, but so also can a herdspersons' cooperative.

I am not a biological ecologist. As a result, the illustrations of the tragedy of the commons that I use in my class discussions tend to be social rather than biological in nature. But one of the Institute Fellows, Fr. Andy Szebenyi, prepared a wonderful analysis of world ecology and economic justice for the Institute session that focused on the long-term ecological consequences of current first- and third-world patterns of material distribution and consumption. I now augment my illustrations with Andy's handout. The handout and the discussions it gives rise to have had the effect of breaking down overly rigid distinctions between the biological and social sciences. This is especially valuable for nonsocial science majors in SOC 101 who may be taking the only social science course of their college careers. It also reinforces a recognition that the tragedy of the commons is very real and that the message of the story is increasingly relevant to citizens of the first and third worlds. The discussion of the tragedy of the commons and Andy's analysis also dovetail with materials dealt with in Andy's course, "Life and Science," a course designed to help humanities, social science, and business majors fulfill their natural science core requirements. Thus, there is at least incipient coordination in the materials presented in two high enrollment biological and social science courses.

Stratification

A standard topic in any introductory sociology course is social stratification, the study of the different institutional systems by which rewards (positive and negative) such as power, prestige, and income are allocated. We study caste stratification systems, market systems, and centrally planned stratification systems. We also focus substantial attention on the roles played by gender, race and ethnicity, and the family in the process of stratification in contemporary America. Finally, we analyze various theories of stratification, in particular, Marxian theory and functionalist theory, the latter being a sociological version of neoclassical economic labor market theory. One of the major readings for the Institute was the American bishops' pastoral letter, *Economic Justice for All*. I decided to finish our analysis of social stratification by having the students read essential parts of the pastoral letter before discussing it as a theory and as a political statement on stratification. I noted in class that because well over seventy percent of Le Moyne students have indicated in surveys that they are Roman Catholics, the bishops' letter bore at least some relation to them. The discussion of Marx and the bishops, and Milton Friedman and the bishops, was lively, powerful, and productive.

Concepts of value

In SOC 101 we treat the anthropological concept of culture in great detail. Central to an understanding of culture as the symbol system through which groups organize and construct their perceptions and understandings of the social and physical worlds is the concept of "value." Used anthropologically, the concept of value refers to group, institution, or society-specific abstract standards of the good, the bad, the beautiful, the ugly, the sacred, the profane, etc.

Barron Boyd, a political scientist and Institute Fellow, prepared a wonderful handout comparing the standards (i.e. values) by which economic value is measured among the Botswana of southern Africa and within the American market economy. The Botswana basically set prices based on need, that is, the asking price of a cow or other good or service is determined by the owner's need at the time of the transaction. While such a system may give rise to apparent inequities in any given transaction, each transaction is part of a larger exchange network that in the long term promotes group-level equality and solidarity, the latter being a prerequisite for survival among subsistance or near-subsistence groups. The American market economy is clearly based on a very different set of values. I use Barron's handout, a handout that he uses in his own courses, to supplement my own cross-cultural examples of the concept of value. It allows me to demonstrate that *economic systems* and their underlying cultural values vary considerably among groups, that they are malleable, and that our own "market economy" is but one among many possible systems. This is an important lesson because it reinforces an appreciation for other cultures—an explicit objective of the Le Moyne College core curriculum. The Botswana/market economy comparison is also important if the students are to consider seriously the value of "economic justice" and the changes that may be necessary in the American economic system if this value is to be encouraged. To consider change, one must be able to conceive of alternatives and possess some degree of respect for these alternatives. Barron's handout helps students to develop this ability.

In my discussion of the Institute itself, I focused substantial attention on group exercises, role playing and other nontraditional (at least for me) pedagogical approaches. These exercises led me to explore a second type of adaptation in my teaching. Below I outline illustrations of the results of my exposure to these alternative approaches to teaching.

Poletown Lives

In the fall of 1988, I taught "Law, Society and Social Science" (SOC 321). The course seeks to develop a social scientific understanding of legal symbols and institutional systems from a cross-cultural perspective. Substantial emphasis is also placed on understanding how legal institutions interact with other institutions such as the family and the economy, and how legal systems change historically. Finally, we analyze central legal concepts such as due process, the rule of law, property rights, and constitutionalism from historical and cross-cultural perspectives. To analyze the issue of property rights I organized a group exercise around a film titled Poletown Lives.

In the early 1980s, a period during which I lived in Detroit, the city was embroiled in a major controversy surrounding the city's efforts to condemn nearly 1,500 homes and other buildings in a neighborhood called Poletown. The cleared site was to be used to build a new and highly automated GM Cadillac assembly plant. Financially burdened, the city sought to preserve auto jobs and the economic advantages such a plant are thought to provide. The city had lost thousands of auto-related jobs during the past decade to other states and to foreign countries. The residents of Poletown, many of them retired auto workers and their families, were utterly shocked that the city, through its Economic Redevelopment Commission, would want to and could, in fact, summarily condemn their homes, hospitals, stores, schools, and worst of all, their churches, for the project. A full-scale battle, complete with boycotts, demonstrations, court hearings and appeals, and widespread press coverage took place. The issues, of course, were complex; but in essence they pitted economic redevelopment for the city as a whole, based on the goal of retaining the auto industry in Detroit, against the rights of a community to exist and the rights of individuals to maintain private property even against the large-scale, but nonetheless private, interests of GM as expressed by the city. Ultimately, GM and the city prevailed and the Cadillac plant was built.

Poletown Lives is an award-winning film that chronicles the events of the Poletown vs. GM controversy from the perspective of the community. The exercise that I developed around the film and the Poletown controversy involved the following elements. All students were given written materials concerning the controversy, including the nearly fifty page Michigan State Supreme Court decision that allowed the city to use the power of eminent domain to take property for the project; an article for the *Washington and Lee Law Review* that analyzed the Court's decision; a *Harvard Business Review* article that analyzed the ethical dimensions of the case; and an extensive collection of clippings from the Detroit and national press. Next we watched the film during a class period. In the following class period, we spent about twenty minutes discussing the film and clarifying factual matters raised in the reading. In the remaining time, I divided the class into the following groups for the purpose of holding a rehearing of the appeals case before the Michigan Supreme Court: representatives of the City of Detroit, representatives of the Poletown Civic Association, representatives of GM, representatives of the United Auto Workers, representatives of the Diocese of Detroit, and the three judges of the Court. Each group was given five days, including a weekend, to prepare for the retrial. On the day of the hearing each group was given five minutes to present its arguments, and then the judges were given fifteen minutes to pose questions to the parties. The judges then retired to make their decision. They found in favor of the Poletown community, thus reversing the lower court's ruling in favor of the city. In the next class period, we spent about twenty minutes debriefing.

Student reaction to the Poletown exercise was extremely positive, based on comments made at the debriefing session and in the final course evaluations. My sense is also that the exercise helped students to appreciate the proposition that property is not so much an object as it is a set of socially constructed and sustained rights that are established and altered through the political process. My sense is that the students also developed a heightened awareness of just how complex the issue of economic development really is in terms of its community and political consequences. Finally, I believe that we jointly developed a sense of the importance of involvement in the legal and political process, a sense that echoed one elderly Poletown resident's lament that her only regret about her actions in the protests was that she had not become more actively involved in the Poletown resistance earlier. I suspect that there is little need to sketch out the parallel between the Poletown exercise and the Summer Institute exercises that I described earlier.

The _Rutgers Law Review_ exercise

Toward the end of the "Law, Society and Social Science" course, I wanted to draw the students more actively into the process of legal policy development, implementation, and evaluation. (In this regard it is notable that at least fifteen of the twenty students in the class intended to go on to law school.) For some years I have done research with a colleague, Sarah Ramsey, on the legal system's provision of attorneys to represent children in protection proceedings. In 1988, we published the last of seven articles on this topic in the _Rutgers Law Review_. The article was an effort to summarize what we had found over the years and to make a series of very specific proposals for improving the representation of children in these cases.

I frequently include one of my own articles in the syllabi of my more specialized upper-division courses. I suppose my motivation is partly egotistic, but I have always thought that students, when they pay our salaries, are paying not just for the teaching we do, but also for our research which they should have the opportunity to see and evaluate. One of the problems I have encountered in attempting to generate discussions about my own research is that students become extremely deferential and find it difficult to criticize the content of the articles. My guess is that this problem derives in part from an overdeveloped respect for the printed word and in part from an overdeveloped respect for teachers. Because one of the major goals in any course I teach is to develop students' ability to critically assess the outputs of public policy analysis and social science, over the years I have searched for better methods to generate critical discussions of primary reading, especially when the reading is my own work.

One of the lessons that I learned from the role-playing exercises at the Summer Institute is that, far from being a confining experience, taking on a new role, as dictated by the rules of an exercise, may actually set one free to do things that one might not ordinarily be able, or imagine oneself being able, to do. This is an odd lesson for a sociologist to learn mid-career. After all, role theory, one of the building blocks of sociological theory, has long analyzed precisely the processes that I have referred to above. In any case, I decided to address the problem of extreme deference by tinkering with the prescriptions and proscriptions of our roles as teacher and students in the discussion of the *Rutgers Law Review* article.

I told the students in SOC 321 that there was very little point in my lecturing about the article. My co-author and I had analyzed our data, discussed our findings, drawn our conclusions, and made our policy recommendations as best we could. Hence, for purposes of discussion I noted that I had nothing to add to the article by way of exposition. I pointed out, however, that as is common in legal and policy analysis, the views we expressed were far from uniformly accepted. Indeed, more than a few people in and out of government disagreed with us on several issues. I did not reveal what these issues were. I asked the students to prepare for our class discussion of the Rutgers article by taking on the role of critic. That is, the students were to avoid making any favorable comments on the article and, instead, were to prepare two or three critical questions for me about what was argued in the article. The questions could pursue any line of attack: statistical, methodological, logical, legal, moral, etc. My job was to attempt, as best I could, to respond. The students did a very solid job. The questions they raised were as good or better than most of those raised by journal reviewers and commentators at professional meetings. I had the sense that because their job was to critique, the members of the class read the article much more closely than they had read most of the other readings in the course. I also sensed that they felt very liberated by the rules of the exercise. And I believe they simply had a good time "going after me." Finally, I am quite certain that subsequent to the exercise, the class members were much more at ease in critically analyzing our readings, my lectures, and our discussions.

Again, as in the Poletown exercise, I found myself using *role-playing* exercises to alter my style of teaching and my students' style of classroom work. The responses that I received concerning these exercises and my own evaluations of them were very positive, and I attribute much of this benefit to my experience of the Institute.

Conclusion

In this personal reflection I have attempted to recount who I was as a teacher and a social scientist prior to the 1988 Summer Institute, the experiences of the Institute that were most meaningful to me, and how I have adapted my approach to teaching based on these experiences. I have very positive feelings about the Institute and the Values Program. My hope is that this commentary provides a meaningful description and analysis of the bases for these feelings.

Endnote

1. See *Accent on Improving College Teaching and Learning* (1989, Ann Arbor, MI: University of Michigan).

6

A Mathematician's Perspective

The Itinerary

Here is a map of this commentary, a guide that highlights its ethos. It begins with a personal story that, though somewhat discursive, helps explain the tone and objectives of the commentary.

A few years ago, a student in one of my classes asked a (mathematical) question that led me on a long investigation. Though I was able to answer the student's question quickly enough, answering it was like cutting off one of Hydra's heads—multiple new ones materialized on the same body. Related questions haunted me long after the inquisitive student had graduated. Finally one day, during one of my periodic bouts with these questions, I made what seemed a major breakthrough. Excited by my discovery and reasonably convinced of its novelty, I enshrined it in a paper and submitted the paper to a professional journal. Unfortunately, I missed (by a mere seventy-five years) being the first to achieve the breakthrough. Although that was the death knell for the paper as a research contribution, a particularly sympathetic referee encouraged me to revise the paper as an expository work and provided me with helpful suggestions for doing so. Since the editor of the journal echoed the referee's encouragement, I substantially revised the paper and resubmitted it. Here is a portion of what the friendly referee had to say about the revision.

> You [the editor] write that comparison with the previous version of the paper is unimportant. Here, therefore, it is. That earlier version was written with self-conscious loving care and enthusiasm by a man who had, apparently, discovered the salient facts for himself, who had been delighted with them, and who wanted the world not only to be offered his discoveries but also to notice them. This new version is written by a scholar who knows the whole field, loves it, and wants other people to love it too. Some of the attractiveness of the earlier version is lost. That is sad, but perhaps inevitable. On the other hand, the present paper is significantly shorter, somewhat easier, very much smoother, and full of the relevant information about other scholars' contributions that was missing from the earlier version. I am sorry that my suggestions have led to a loss of naivete and charming freshness, but I am gratified to have come across an author who takes my suggestions seriously.

(After a second revision in which I tried to restore some of the "freshness" of the original, the paper was accepted for publication.)

The relevance of the story is this. For me, the Summer Institute unlocked a treasure trove of new discoveries, fresh insights, and different perspectives. These are probably not globally original—this commentary does not belong in the *Chronicle of Higher Education*—but they were and are personal break- throughs. I am delighted with them. As the referee perceptively recognized in my paper, I want people not only to be offered my discoveries but to notice them. I want people to feel my enthusiasm, to find a "charming freshness" in what I express, even to glimpse my naïveté.

To give the illusion of structure, I have divided the remainder of this tale into five sections. The first reveals some of the biases, presuppositions, and general baggage that I brought with me into the Institute; the next three attempt to unravel (what for me were) the three main strands of the Institute; and the last looks at residual effects of the Institute. In the three middle sections, I try to speak in more general language, emphasizing aspects of the Institute that were probably common to most participants. In the last section, I concentrate on specific illustrations unique to me.

Two caveats are in order. First, this is as much a story about me as it is about the Summer Institute. While observations are always dependent on the observer, this is especially true here. Second, unraveled strands lose the synergistic benefits, the gestalt, of their natural interwoven state. This account suffers from the defect of all reductionist approaches—it slights those properties that emerge only at the level of a fully operational system.

Baggage Check

As Teilhard de Chardin put it so eloquently: "Is not the peculiar difficulty of every synthesis that its end is already implicit in its beginnings?" What I left the Institute with was intimately related to what I went in with.

The Summer Institute came at a propitious time in my life. Winds of personal change were anomalously gusty then. In the two years prior to the Institute, I took leading roles in two community organizations; participated (for the first time) in a variety of groups structured around the theme of personal growth; ended a fifteen-year estrangement from organized religion by joining a Unitarian society; discovered humanistic psychology; radically redefined my relationship with my wife (we are now divorced); was granted tenure; successfully adopted carpentry as a hobby; began experimenting with small-group strategies in teaching my mathematics classes; and developed into a full-time parent.

Inherent in all of this tumult was a considerable amount of re-evaluation—of self-image, of personal goals, of accepted norms and conventional wisdom. One result was that I was unusually (by my standards) open to new ideas and perspectives. Another was that my general level of excitement was high. Perhaps most significantly, I was increasingly accepting of and comfortable with myself. I was and am still learning to become a good friend to myself.

This personal awakening invigorated my teaching. I found myself more empathetic to my students, more able to feel the discomfort and pain of their struggles, more appreciative of their talents, abilities, and potential. (This is hardly surprising—I was more appreciative of my *own* struggles, pain, talents, abilities, and potential.) Though I have always basically liked my students, they have frequently irritated me with their habits, beliefs, and general immaturity. The year preceding the Institute saw a major shift in my attitudes. Students became much more human for me. I entered the Summer Institute as a teacher who had (at least from my own reference point) recently and dramatically reconceptualized his pedagogical framework.

My professional rejuvenation had one glaring deficiency. Prior to the beginning of the Summer Institute, I knew few faculty members outside my department. In fact, somewhat incredibly, I had never spoken more than a couple of times to any of the other eighteen participants of the Institute. I regarded myself as shy, and my departmental niche was a very pleasant one that met my immediate social needs. However, my reclusive behavior at work was increasingly incongruent with my overall approach to social interactions. An eruption was brewing; and, as I realized when I first heard of it, the Summer Institute was the perfect vent. Thus, despite a modicum of apprehension, I entered the Institute with clear determination to get to know and be known by my peers.

In addition to the three large bags I just checked—a general spirit of adventure in my life, a renewed sense of myself as a teacher, and the anticipation of joining a fellowship with my colleagues—I brought two pieces of carry-on luggage. The first was a long-standing interest in economic justice, stemming largely from my two years as a Peace Corps volunteer. The other was the thrill of being a student again, this time in a stimulating honors class outside my major field. There was, of course, other baggage rooted more deeply in my socio-cultural background; but that is the subject of a later section.

There is a final important point. Though baggage slows and hinders travel, it also supports the traveler. Whatever impediments it created, my personal baggage prepared me to engage actively in the Summer Institute, to invest myself in it, and to share responsibility for its outcome. As it turned out, I had packed well.

Take Off: Values Education

From its inception, the Summer Institute was organized around the idea of values education. In fact, if forced to describe the Summer Institute in a single sentence, I would say, "It was a faculty development program designed to enhance the quality of values education." There is one problem with this one-liner, a problem that bares the very kernel of the Summer Institute: Just what *is* values education? In this section, I'll give my interpretation. This will, I hope, serve two purposes. On one hand, by enunciating my current understanding of values education, I go a long way toward explaining what I think the Summer Institute (and its parent, the Values Program) is all about. On the other, by documenting how markedly my understanding grew—it was at ground zero before the Institute—I testify to the Institute's efficacy.

It was in connection with the Summer Institute that I first heard the term "values education." The phrase aroused more my suspicions than my interest. Up to that point in my life, the overwhelming majority of people who had spoken to me of values had done so: 1) in the context of converting others to theirs, and 2) as though values were static principles of eternal and universal truth. I find both of these approaches repugnant. In addition, I was wary that Le Moyne's religious heritage as a Catholic institution might exert undue influence on the definition of values education. As an agnostic still in rebellion against the dogma of my Methodist upbringing, I was in no mood to be party to some camouflaged form of catechism.

It was, therefore, a relief when Richard Morrill (initial facilitator and keynote speaker for the Institute) propounded a view of values education (or, as he preferred to call it, "educating for values") that was neither doctrinaire nor sectarian. The points of his theory that I assimilated were:

1. Values comprise not a set of rules for conduct, but rather predispositions that orient decision making. We all value some things more than others.

2. Values are part of a feedback loop; there is a two-way interactive effect between values and the decisions they orient.

3. Indoctrination is not a tool of authentic values education; to the contrary, values education uses open inquiry to encourage self-reflection; it succeeds by gently and lovingly fomenting internal (that is, with a person's own value structure) dissonance.

4. *All* education, whether acknowledged as such or not, is value-suffused; thus, the question is not whether we choose to educate for values, but rather whether we choose to do so with awareness and intentionality.

5. Values education depends on dialogue; teachers must act as affirming mentors for human discovery, not as judging minions of sealed truths; they must be as skilled at listening as at talking, as prepared to learn from students as to share knowledge with them.

The theory that Morrill expounded supplied a valuable framework, a helpful schematic diagram of values education.[1] But just as people do not become carpenters by merely poring over blueprints (however helpful blueprints may be to carpenters), so people do not become values educators by merely studying Dr. Morrill's theories. Would-be carpenters begin as apprentices to accomplished carpenters; they learn carpentry by doing it in actual construction projects. The same holds for would-be values educators, which is precisely the raison d'être of the Summer Institute.

Master values educator Ken Dolbeare guided us as we built a fully functioning scale model of a values-centered class. We used real materials—readings about economic justice and concomitant topics; real tools—small groups, role playing, round-table discussions (held around a square table), varied physical settings, and mock hearings; and real blood, sweat, toil, and tears (the first and last, as far as I know, only figurative!)

Unlike carpentry apprentices, we trained for only twelve days. For that reason, we did not dwell on easily developed skills for which there are many good references. We spent only limited time on the pedagogical equivalents of learning to drive a nail, saw a board, or chisel a joint. Instead we focused on developing an overall sense of the craft: where are the potential trouble spots? What are the main stages of construction? When does one use which general strategies? How can one tell whether the project is on schedule or not? What are the acceptable tolerance ranges for various procedures?

Inherent in values education is conflict. Indeed, it is one of the driving forces. There are three major areas of conflict that I noticed at the Institute.

First, there was a tension between content and process. For teachers facing a jam-packed course syllabus, the notion of using a values-education approach poses a dilemma. Using such an approach involves an apparent sacrifice of content in the name of lofty but diaphanous goals. We bumped against this conflict frequently during the Summer Institute. Lurking in this conflict is a fundamental question voiced by one of the participants: just what is essential in what we teach? Also lurking is an equally fundamental question: can content and process exist independently of one another? Given proper consideration, these simple questions shake the very core of our educational institutions and practices, which is why it was so important that we were investigating them at the Institute.

Second, there was a deep epistomological conflict that surfaced often. In various guises it revolved around this question: how do people with different approaches to the pursuit of truth and knowledge communicate effectively and make joint decisions? Consider, for instance, the problem of "rating" the merit of values education. There is an aspect to values education that confounds attempts to measure (with conventional means) the depth and span of its effects. On one hand, values education requires substance, a topic for discussion, observational data; it cannot operate in a vacuum. In this respect, values education is like all forms of education. However, values education goes far beyond an attempt to impart "objective" knowledge; it focuses on the way the knowledge is processed, integrated, and synthesized. The goals of values education go beyond filling files in the mind. They aim to reorganize, on an ongoing basis, the entire filing system, and in fact to inspire a self-perpetuating process of reorganization. As a result, traditional schemas underrate the contributions of values education on two counts. For one, they tend to credit education with filling the files, but to credit the individual with reorganizing them. For the second, tests, the standard for rating educational success, dwell almost exclusively on "file-folder" knowledge, and therefore ignore the major benefit of a values-education approach.

This difficulty surfaces in evaluating the Summer Institute itself. In assessing its effectiveness, the natural tendency is to ask participants: what concrete facts did you learn about economic justice? What specific techniques did you learn about teaching for values? As academics, we are used to viewing knowledge quantitatively and pragmatically, with the expectation that educational progress can be authoritatively documented. Questions like: How has your conceptual framework for thinking about economic justice changed? How are your beliefs about values education different? How were you affected as a person? strike us as a bit too nebulous and subjective to serve as proper evaluative tools. We need "proof" that important business transpired; intuition and gut feelings are insufficient. I do not mean to imply that it is wrong to evaluate the Summer Institute logically and objectively; I would be a traitor to my discipline if I did. I *do* mean that there are limits to what objective analysis will reveal about the potency of the Institute. Many of the issues addressed at the Institute are untidy, sprawling, and slippery. We did not resolve them, but we engaged them wholeheartedly. The authenticity of our struggle, more than any quantifiable outcome, is what made the Summer Institute so critically important to the promulgation of values-centered education.

This second conflict also manifests itself in the schism, both philosophical and operational, between teachers of science and of humanities. The Institute attracted only one natural scientist.

A central reason is the widespread belief among scientists (at least at Le Moyne, and probably elsewhere) that science courses offer few opportunities to address values issues. The simplistic motto: "Values in humanities; facts in science" summarizes a common attitude. Even among nonscientists at the Institute, there was skepticism about the applicability of values education outside the humanities and social sciences. To some of us (I fall into this camp), science is so suffused with values that it is fertile ground for values education; to others, science is sufficiently value-free as to be inherently divorced from values education. Different people regard scientific knowledge differently. The trick, well managed at the Institute, is to promote dialogue so that people in both camps (and the many people falling between the two extreme camps) can learn, grow, and change.

Finally, there was a critical conflict that remained almost totally submerged, nothing but its tip bobbing occasionally above the surface. In deference to my carpentry allegory, I have called it the "working on our own house" controversy. To my mind, the significant differentiating factor among participants in the Institute was neither their backgrounds nor their disciplines, but rather their willingness to practice on their own houses. Values education, I came to realize, does not respect the distinction between subject and object; nor does it recognize academic rank and advanced degrees. At its best, it is a process that, for *every* individual involved, is both involutionary and evolutionary, a process that relies on both introspection and social engagement. Because of this, values education is not an entirely comfortable experience, particularly for those of us whose professional cloaks are convenient and well-accepted shields against the subversive tendencies of dialogical education. Effective facilitators of values education cannot insulate themselves from the electricity of the approach; their expertise helps ground the process, but only if they are willing to accept the shocks it generates. Of its promoters, values education demands continual and critical *self-examination*; in return it offers abundant opportunity to build and help others build.

For me, the power and beauty of the Summer Institute lay in the fact that it was not merely *about* values education—it *was* values education. We learned primarily from direct experience, and experiential learning has a potency unrivaled by other forms of learning.

Meeting My Fellow Passengers: The Chance to Build Community

So ubiquitous has the phrase "build community" become, so broad its meaning, that I use it with misgivings. Indeed, the statement, "The Summer Institute really helped to build community at Le Moyne," is true, but generically so. Substitute any process or activity for "Summer Institute" and any group or organization for "Le Moyne" and the statement remains true. In this section, I want to sharpen the meaning of the statement, to reveal what it means to *me*. What kind of community did the Institute help to build and how did it help build it?

Community building is a hot item these days because it bucks one of modern society's most virulent trends: the drive toward separation, fragmentation, and compartmentalization. Nowhere more than in academia do we encounter this trend. On campuses we find a rigidly defined departmental structure that separates learning into prescribed compartments. Nonmixing of faculty is a rule that applies not only interdepartmentally, but increasingly intradepartmentally. The end-state, from which many institutions seem not far removed, is a consortium of independent scholars connected to each other only by the common signature on their paychecks, and coordinated in their activities only by the economic market forces that dictate efficient resource allocation. And the fragmentation we see in our faculties is reflected in myriad other ways. Colleges consist not of people, but of professors, students, administrators, and staff. Students live two distinct lives, academic and nonacademic. Learning is neatly packaged (often freeze-dried) into independent fifteen-week modules called courses, and these courses can then be assembled according to standard recipes to produce majors, minors, freshmen, sophomores, juniors, seniors, and a whole gallery of different degrees. And dualistic attitudes defend the great (false) dichotomies: applied vs. theoretical, intuitive vs.

logical, personal vs. professional, science vs. humanities, social science vs. physical science, researcher vs. teacher.

The Institute built community by reminding us in a visceral way that we faculty members, however dissimilar the methodologies of our disciplines, are engaged in a shared activity that freely crosses departmental boundaries. The Institute built community by repeating a positive feedback loop: we learned from and about each other, which fostered a feeling of trust and mutual respect, which in turn freed us to learn even more from and about each other. The Institute built community by exposing us to our broader selves in each other's presence; "forced" by curiosity, interest, and excitement, we dropped a lot of our role-dominated behavior. The Institute built community by opening us to the enriching potential of our diversity. We learned that, although initially our different voices can produce caoophony, if we keep working at it, those same voices can produce rich and beautiful harmony. The Institute built community by encouraging anastamosis within the network we form together, by dredging new channels for the flow of information and ideas, by enhancing our capability for internal communication. In short, the Institute built community by catalyzing a biological reaction—true dialogue—that defies the law of entropy: it procedes spontaneously, releases vast quantities of energy, yet leaves the reactants even more highly organized and energetic.

There is another dimension to community building: the small day-to-day changes that occur when people feel more comfortable with the people around them. It is in this dimension that community building reveals itself most graphically. However, we shall wait to enter this dimension, for its gateway lies in the last section on effects of the Institute.

Collecting Souvenirs:
Facts and Artifacts from the Institute

Though the Institute comprised a host of intangible aspects, it also included some very tangible ones. Each of the seven main works from the reading list contributed substantially to what I know about economic justice and pedagogical practice. I was dreadfully ignorant of the historical and political roots of current attitudes toward economics and justice when the Institute began. For instance, I knew essentially nothing about the populist movement of the last century until we read and discussed *The Populist Movement* by Lawrence Goodwyn. The discovery of how deeply the issues raised in the *Federalist Papers* affect our national psyche some two hundred years later startled me. From reading and discussing the penetrating analysis of U.S. culture supplied by *Habits of the Heart,* I was left shaking my head at how much of what is all around me (even *in* me!) I had never noticed. In *Pedagogy of the Oppressed* I found an impressive, well-articulated philosophical foundation for my own beliefs about education.

Many (all?) of my colleagues were far better informed than I. For them, the readings probably held fewer surprises and revelations. However, I suspect that the probing inquiry to which our discussions subjected the readings revealed new details for all. When the same artifact undergoes the scrutiny of historians, economists, biologists, philosophers, mathematicians, sociologists, and political scientists, it is bound to yield more of its secrets. This is especially true if, as was the case at the Institute, the scrutiny takes place in an atmosphere of heightened sensitivity to hidden biases, unstated assumptions, and cultural egoism.

The selected readings were rich ground for exploration, but valuable finds occurred elsewhere, too. Individual participants were frequently moved to photocopy and distribute relevant material to the group. In addition, a considerable amount of information was exchanged during the formal and informal Institute discussions. This was particularly true with regard to pedagogical practice. Frequently, a person's remarks would contain oblique reference to a classroom technique. Either privately or publicly, others would press for more details about the technique. Even when such references received no immediate attention, I believe that they helped encourage future experimentation. We were all, I think, surprised at just how much innovative teaching already takes place at Le Moyne. There is an important implication in this: we now know that for friendly sources of help, advice, and inspiraton to improve our teaching, we need look no farther than the faculty lunchroom.

The facilitators of the Institute, in addition to guiding our excavation process, salted the Institute "dig" from their own museums of experience. Ken Dolbeare's description of Evergreen State University and its unorthodox approach to education challenged each of us to question whether our visions of what is possible in the classroom are not unnecessarily narrow. And John Langan infused the Institute with a healthy dose of "real world" applied ethics by drawing on actual work he has done with the banking industry.

There was a great deal that we were not able to unearth during the three weeks of the Institute. Those of us who were not economists before the Institute began were not economists when it ended. None of us left with a revised curriculum or day-to-day lesson plan for our courses in hand. We did not produce a joint critique of the U.S. bishops' pastoral letter on economic justice. Even those discoveries we made that were of obvious worth were, in nearly all instances, still in need of cleaning, cataloging, and complementing. But however incomplete our expedition's search for answers to issues of economic justice and values education, we were working in a prime site with proper equipment and authentic methods. We now know where and how to dig.

Landing and Departure:
Where Did the Trip Take Me?

I like traveling. Trips are exciting, refreshing, and stimulating. Occasionally, they are even more—they are transforming. The Summer Institute was such a trip for me. In this section, I'll describe, by example, some of the transforming aspects. First, however, I need to insert a brief disclaimer. It is impossible to attribute changes sweeping enough to deserve the label "transformation" to a single cause like the Summer Institute. Indeed, adumbrations of most of what I shall report here can be found in the "Baggage Check" section. Moreover, no mathematician worth his salt would ever assert that examples, however numerous, constitute proof of anything more general. I cannot with any validity claim that because *I* experienced certain effects, others would be likely to experience similar effects.

Having *dis*claimed that the Summer Institute's impact was exclusive or universal, I now *pro*claim that the Summer Institute's impact *was* substantial and far-reaching for *me*. A proclamation, of course, has no legitimacy without its "whereas's," so let me supply them. There are three in all. Though there is some encroachment, the first resides in the domain of the classroom, the second, in that of the college community, and the third, in that of the wider world.

In the next few paragraphs, I intend to do more than describe how the Summer Institute affected what I do in my classes. I intend also to answer the (oft-asked) question, "Why would a respectable, level-headed mathematician get mixed up with a fanatical bunch interested in values education?" The first step for both tasks is to give a baseline.

Figuratively speaking, I entered the Institute as a teenaged teacher. I consider my first few years of teaching to be my childhood period, because during that time I faithfully followed the model by which my mathematical parents had reared me. I lectured from a textbook, assigned only "bite-sized" daily exercises from the text, graded primarily according to tests, and treated my subject as a sterile field, uncontaminated by exposure to the subjectivity and ambiguity of history, culture, politics, or (to a large degree) praxis. The aesthetic beauty of an elegant theory, the delicate intricacy of a deep proof, the mental challenge of a beguiling problem, the creative art of searching for patterns, the power of analytical thinking, the thrill and security of living in an abstract world of precision and certainty—these had sufficed to motivate and sustain *me* as a student. That they did not seem to suffice for *my* students shocked me, and eventually propelled me to my (teaching) adolescence.

By the time of the Summer Institute, I had accepted new responsibility as a teacher. No longer content as a traditional explicator of abstruse mathematical notions, I had begun experimenting with different methods of pedagogy. In 1985 (three years before the Institute), a new course ("Introduction to Mathematical Reasoning") that I designed and taught became the required entry-level course for mathematics majors. The version of this course that I taught just prior to the Institute had no text, few lectures, a great deal of small-group work, a flexible contract grading system, and a scheme of problem assignments in which each student did five individually selected mini-projects during the semester. I was, as I said above, a teenager—discovering unexpected new worlds, growing in unpredictable spurts, rebelling (often with giddy enthusiasm) against conventional wisdom, having difficulty settling on a role, and feeling (at those deeper levels often submerged beneath the surface of consciousness) a confusing mix of defiant persistence, apprehension, passion, and isolation. My attempts to behave differently in the classroom were sometimes awkward and uncomfortable; my confidence waxed and waned dramatically; and I had a teenager's knack for juxtaposing genius and lunacy. (Fortunately, I was spared acne and hormone shifts!)

What I needed, and what the Institute provided me, was a well-facilitated group therapy session with other teenaged teachers, a session which gave me positive reinforcement for past accomplishments and present intentions, intriguing ideas for future improvements, and a model, both philosophical and practical, of adult teaching. To put it another way, the Institute helped me understand better *what* I am trying to do, helped me figure out *how* to do it better, and helped me articulate the reasons *why* I want to be doing it. Here are some specific examples of the changes that occurred after the Institute.

From Toys to Trial. For a long time before the Institute, I had toyed with the following idea for illustrating mathematical concepts (like assumptions, definitions, and logical inferences). Pick a contemporary, controversial, social issue (say the U.S. response to apartheid), and have students participate in a debate. Then have them try to analyze what went on in the debate in terms of mathematical concepts. Such an exercise would, I hoped, not only illustrate mathematical concepts in a lively manner; it would also raise important questions about the limitations of mathematical approaches. The idea sat dormant until, during the Institute, I found myself involved in a role-playing exercise and debate. The very next semester, I stopped toying with the idea and tried it (with pleasing results).

Between Autocracy and Anarchy. In attempting to be semi-democratic in class, I had developed a habit of opening many classes with the question, "What would you like to work on today?" The response was usually silence, so I took over. By watching what went on in the Institute, I realized that voting requires a ballot. Now I continue to ask for student input in shaping the class agenda, but by presenting three or four options. It works much better. Elsewhere, too, the Institute made me realize (in a way that I can *use*) that there is a subtle but important distinction between sharing power and abdicating leadership.

Speaking Up. Just before the Institute commenced, I had agreed to help two other members of the department teach a "History of Mathematics" course. This was novel in a number of senses. The course was new to Le Moyne; it came in response to a student initiative; I had never team-taught before; and my knowledge of the history of mathematics was limited to knowing the names of a few mathematicians whose names were borne by theorems. Nonetheless, I took a lead in planning the format for the course; and my format was based on ideas from the Institute. In particular, students selected and presented nearly all the material, and there were long discussions about the societal implications of various mathematical developments. One of the two colleagues on the team was a participant in the 1989 Summer Institute. Recently he remarked to me. "Bill, at the time I didn't understand a lot of what you were trying to do with that 'History of Mathematics' class. Now I do!"

Speaking Out. The spring following the Institute, I wrote and presented a paper on the "Introduction to Mathematical Reasoning" course at a regional mathematics conference. Though I might have done so regardless of the Institute, I certainly did so with greater conviction, confidence, and cohesion because of the Institute.

The examples proffered thus far give me one excuse, a very utilitarian one, for consorting with known perpetrators of values education: Understanding the *methodology* of values education makes me a more effective teacher of mathematical content.

This is no mere coincidence. There is a large overlap in the abilities mathematical and values education seek to develop— thinking critically and analytically; recognizing deeper patterns; ferreting out internal inconsistencies; deciding what aspects of a given problem are salient; identifying hidden assumptions and implicit definitions; learning to write ideas in crisp, cogent fashion; forming and testing conjectures; and searching for new ways of understanding old experience. Indeed, abandoning any pretense at modesty, I can point to my own contributions at the Institute as evidence for the similarity between the ends of mathematical and values education. With nary a philosophy, history, religion, sociology, or political science course anywhere in my undergraduate or graduate transcripts, I was nonetheless able to participate actively and productively in the Institute. In further support of this utilitarian excuse, I would mention that the kind of methods I have tried in my courses are receiving a great deal of attention within the mainstream mathematical community.

I claim professional ethics as further exculpation for my involvement in the Summer Institute. This excuse is likely to be more controversial than the first, because, unlike the first, it speaks of the *content* of values education in mathematics classes. In the words of one of yesteryear's leaders, I want to make one thing perfectly clear. *Whether* to introduce values into mathematics classes is not at issue—they are already there, everywhere. The mathematics we teach is inextricably linked to Western thought. It values one way of knowing almost exclusively. (Mystics do not fare well in mathematics classes!) Favoritism is rampant: for elegant solutions, for tidy theories, for quantitative aspects of problems, for hard clean edges, for certainty and precision. Moreover, mathematical biases have metastisized into our culture; people follow the ways of winners, and mathematics has a great track record. All too often we see examples of the epigram, "If we can't measure it, it doesn't exist." In fact, mathematics has so successfully satisfied the human thirst for understanding the world in human terms that it is (paradoxically) no longer seen as a human endeavor. Many people treat it as a god—they fear it, they leave communication with it to the high priests and priestesses of the religions,[2] they regard its utterances as unassailable, and they believe it can work miracles. Beyond question, mathematical values flow into society. Furthermore, the flow is reciprocal, and the reverse flow is not all subterranean. A leading (financial) supporter of mathematical research is the U.S. Department of Defense. This support wields a none-too-subtle influence on which mathematical theories and problems get the most attention. Thus, I find it supremely ironic when I hear "professional" arguments against raising values issues in mathematics classes. If anything, the principle of professional integrity demands *fuller* acknowledgment and discussion of values questions, because they already pervade mathematics.

Finally, I plead moral responsibility to justify my participation in the Institute. Various stereotypes to the contrary, mathematicians are people. As people, mathematicians face the same moral dilemmas as others. The dilemmas range from the splashy—like whether to accept Star Wars money for research (a debate that has raged in the pages of the *Bulletin of the American Mathematical Society* for some time) and how to provide equal opportunity in mathematics to women and people of color—to the mundane—like how to treat a student who has missed a test. In addition, as people, mathematicians suffer the consequences of living in a world where *incredible* numbers of decisions are made upon the recommendations of mathematical models and consultants. The idealist in me regards as folly a system in which managers totally ignorant of mathematical nuances talk to consultants totally ignorant of social values and thereby determine what drugs can be marketed, what plants will be closed, what utility rates should be set, and what weapons systems should be developed. And the realist in me regards as highly improbable that the overall mathematical competence of managers will improve significantly in the foreseeable future. My conclusion is that those taught to use mathematical tools *must* be encouraged to consider how the tools *ought* (in the moral, not mathematical, sense) to be used. It sounds a bit melodramatic, but to my way of thinking, blind obedience to mathematical authority is no more allowable as a defense for making imprudent decisions than blind obedience to military authority was for making immoral ones at Nuremburg.

My awareness that professional and moral responsibilities are interrelated predated the Summer Institute. But the awareness greatly intensified during the Institute and assumed far more cogency in determining my actions. As a person, I have a value system; as an authority figure (in the classroom), the values I exhibit *do* serve as models for my students. Moreover, *however* I choose to act in the classroom, *some* values come across. I want to underscore this point. Even if I do my best to separate my personal values from my professional behavior, I *am* modeling a value—that of compartmentalizing personality according to role-specific behavior. As it turns out, I am no longer so enamored of that particular value, so it doesn't make sense that I should be modeling it.

In other words, the Institute helped me realize just how skimpy a cloak academic objectivity really is. I gradually came to recognize what now seems obvious: there is no way I can avoid revealing what *I* value highly as I teach. This recognition entails considerable new responsibility—I now give a great deal of thought to just which parts of my value system are most appropriate to expose—but also considerable new freedom—the freedom to be more spontaneous, authentic, and whole when I am teaching.

Here is a specific example where I made a conscious decision to model nonmathematical values. One year, classes began at Le Moyne earlier than at my then four-year-old son's nursery school. There were four class periods during which I had the joint responsibilities of parent and teacher. I could have found a baby-sitter to care for my son, but I decided to take him to class with me instead. There were two main reasons. First, I wanted my students to see a public demonstration of a father providing nurturance. Second, I wanted to illustrate parental duties being given the same status as professional ones. Far from disrupting the class, my son's presence seemed to promote a freer and more relaxed learning environment. I think I seemed more human and approachable to my students.

I could go on, but this proclamation is already dangerously long; time for the second whereas, focusing on the college community. This is the realm in which the Institute's effects on me were most explosive. Since I was such a recluse before the Institute, this is hardly surprising. Yet I think it would be a mistake to regard my experience as a mere anomaly caused by the severity of my previous isolation. In my opinion, the Institute's greatest strength was its ability to forge new bonds and channels of communication among members of the college community. I remember reading somewhere that human intelligence is correlated less with the size of the brain than with the density of its convolutions and interconnections. Whether this is true or not, it ought to be. The greater the number of feedback loops, the more responsive and efficient a system is. What makes the Summer Institute so attractive is that it is the ideal developmental program—it uses a relatively small external stimulus to provoke a large, internally sustaining response. The Institute did not so much give us new resources as it gave us new ways of using the resources we already have in abundance. For instance:

During the first week of the Summer Institute, I discovered that fellow participant Bob Kelly, of the Sociology Department, like me, is a jogger. To borrow a line from *Casablanca*, "It was the start of a beautiful relationship." Running at lunchtime during the Institute, we had enjoyable and fruitful discussions of the proceedings. After the Institute, we continued our joint runs and conversations. I have learned a great deal of sociology, gotten in better shape, and made a good friend. Bob and I now see each other often socially so our five-year-old sons can play while we sip wine. We also share pedagogical information. Bob gave me several ideas that I have incorporated in my courses. In addition, we have discussed preliminary ideas for revising the statistics course taught by the mathematics department to social scientists, with an eye toward team-teaching next year.

I got to know Bruce Shefrin (Political Science) the second week of the Institute. It was just at the time my wife and I had decided to separate. Bruce had gone through a separation a couple years before and had a lot of helpful advice. More recently, I began helping Bruce work on the 1991 Summer Institute on science and technology.

John Freie (Political Science) was a person whose ideas I had heard second-hand well before the Summer Institute. My wife had taken his course, "Alternatives in Education," in 1986. Some of his ideas had crept into my classes already. Nothing prevented me from going up to his office and discussing the ideas further face-to-face; yet it was not until I got to know him in the Institute that I did so.

From Don Kirby (Religious Studies), I picked up a technique I used for the first time recently—interviewing each student at the beginning of the course. I've found it invaluable in helping me establish rapport with my classes and in encouraging students to seek individual help when needed. Don, a Jesuit with counseling experience, has also lent me his sympathetic ear on several occasions.

It was not only by enabling me to establish personal contact with colleagues that the Institute helped me integrate more fully into the college community. Immediately following the Institute, I volunteered to become associate director of the Values Program. In doing so, I plugged into a network of people who had committed themselves four years earlier to the ideas I was just discovering with such relish. I also began assisting in the freshman orientation program, leading discussions of the books, *All Quiet on the Western Front* and *Hiroshima.* (The idea for including this activity as part of orientation came from the Institute.) In a similar vein, last spring Bruce Shefrin and I had dinner with twenty students from one of the dorms and discussed issues of economic justice. Janet Bogdan (Sociology), Darryl Anderson (financial aid director), and I showed our old Peace Corps slides to a crowd of 50 education students one night. All of these activities were outgrowths of my association with the Summer Institute.

I could add to the list of examples, but I suspect the list has already grown tedious. I hope it is apparent why I say only half jokingly that since the Summer Institute, I've begun to work on my liberal arts degree. What I hope emerges also is that as I have increased my involvement in the college community, the boundaries between my private, professional, and social lives have dissolved. I no longer have to be three or four different people according to where I am and what I am doing. Corny as it may sound, I've really come to view the college community as a kind of extended family.

I'll keep the last whereas brief, citing just three instances in which the Institute inspired me to action in the wider world. The fall after the Institute, I facilitated a weekend retreat on values for a local environmental group of which I am a member. I based the program entirely on my experience at the Institute. The following spring, I chaired the planning committee for a conference entitled, "Science, Religion, and Environmental Harmony," held at Le Moyne. One of the panelists for the conference, chosen upon my recommendation, was Andrew Szebenyi, a biologist I met at the Institute. Had I not heard Andy speak during the Institute, it never would have occurred to me to recommend him. This past summer, I was recruited to teach a course at Syracuse University for a group of engineers. I decided to use the same methods I use in my courses at Le Moyne. The students (juniors and seniors) reported that it was the first time they had ever experienced anything besides lectures in a mathematics class. That led me to spend some time talking to the chair of the Mathematics Department at Syracuse University (whom I knew fairly well already) about what I was doing and why. Though cautious, he seemed interested. A seed was planted! He promised to look at the course evaluations. I don't know whether he did, but I hope so—they were very favorable, a third of the students commenting that it was the best mathematics class they had ever taken.

That ends the proclamation, and with it, my travelogue. The difference between what I have presented here and what I actually experienced as a member of the 1988 Summer Institute is every bit as great as the difference between a slide show of a trip and the trip itself. You really did have to be there! Still, there is something to be said for snapshots, even those of an amateur photographer using a cheap camera. The mere fact that I—who chose my undergraduate school based on the fact that I would not have to take English composition—was so enchanted as to write a commentary with more prose than my doctoral dissertation has to tell you something about the spell the Summer Institute cast on me!

Endnotes

1. Here and in what follows, I'll speak as if values education were half of a dualistic pair—values education and normal education. Of course, that is absurd, and in direct contradiction to point 4 above. The phrase "values education" should be understood as "an approach that puts greater emphasis than is customary on the five aspects enumerated above."

2. I should add that these attitudes persist in spite of, not because of, the efforts of the high priests and priestesses. Here are pertinent observations by some exceptional mathematicians:

> "[mathematics] is the subject in which we never know what we are talking about nor whether what we are saying is true."—Bertrand Russell

> "As far as the laws of mathematics refer to reality, they are not certain; and as far as they are certain, they do not refer to reality."—Albert Einstein

> "Because our representation of reality is so much easier to grasp than reality itself, we tend to confuse the two and to take our concepts and symbols for reality."—Fritof Capra

> "The actual situation is this. [Mathematical] proofs . . . are established by 'consensus of the qualified.' A real proof is not checkable by a machine, or even by any mathematician not privy to the gestalt, the mode of thought of the particular field of mathematics in which the proof is located. Even to the 'qualifed reader,' there are normally differences of opinion as to whether a real proof (one that is actually spoken or written down) is complete or correct."—Philip Davis and Reuben Hersh in *The Mathematical Experience*

7

Two Student Perspectives

One Student's Perspective

When Fr. Donald Kirby described the Values Program to my religion class in the second semester of my sophomore year, I was interested in its various aims for several personal and perhaps selfish reasons. I had been involved in many different efforts directed toward raising students' awareness of social issues, and this new development seemed a great opportunity for more involvement or leadership. It was also very interesting to me that so many different interest groups could be involved cooperatively in a single program. At the same time, I was excited about the prospect of working to challenge my own and my fellow students' sensibilities to a point where we could take action based on strong and confirmed values.

I was a bit alarmed, though, that the project had come so far in its formative stages without any sort of student input or feedback. I knew of several people in addition to myself who would have been eager to give input and I mentioned them to Fr. Kirby. He informed us that students would be contacted soon with details about a meeting to elicit ideas for future events.

I envisioned the project as a large-scale, long-term effort to educate students about vital contemporary issues, including everything from drug abuse to poverty to racism to war. As I mentioned, it seemed that this project could challenge our values, raising them to new levels of maturity and pushing us to effect positive changes in the world around us.

I was beginning to understand that we students at Le Moyne—predominately middle-class Catholics from New York state—are very sheltered from the many problems and issues that face our world. For the most part, we are fairly conservative and unwilling to make personal sacrifices for the better interests of others. But it is so important that we realize how our decision making, even an individual level, can affect the future of our country and the world. It is vital that we be educated in the issues of personal and social ethics. If this education hasn't already taken place in the home or through high school, isn't it the responsibility of the college or university to fully prepare its graduates for the world? Certainly any college founded in a liberal arts or humanities tradition would say so.

In many ways, I didn't realize how idealistic I was. The prospect of defining values is itself very difficult, let alone the work of challenging fellow students to examine their attitudes and codes of conduct. I had no idea of how huge and complex the project was. But, the hoped-for cooperation among faculty, administration and students seemed to have great potential—one group alone could not be successful in undertaking such an effort.

The initial meeting with the students was fruitful, with at least twenty student leaders participating in a brainstorming session. We focused on different ways to expose students to the Values Program through extracurricular functions including movies, plays, panels, and dinner-discussions. Many of these students shared my enthusiasm for the project's potential, and we were happy to hear that we would be contacted with more information in the Fall semester.

That summer the faculty had their first Summer Institute, focusing on issues of economic justice. Again, I thought it unfortunate that students could not be involved, and this exclusion proved to be a matter for later debate. I believed that student input would have been valuable for shaping the Academic Forum component of the project and for directing the faculty's work toward specific student needs and interests. Those students involved in the Institute could then have provided the leadership for their peers in the student portion of the project, which I will discuss next.

When I returned to school in August, I used my position as chair of the Academic Affairs Committee of the Student Senate to form a student group to work cooperatively with the faculty project. Despite the fact that the Values Group members are among the finest faculty at Le Moyne, they don't have the experience in programming events that the student group could offer. I also thought it would be helpful to have the group generate ideas for Values Program events that would be especially appealing to the rest of the student body. I contacted several students who had seemed interested in the project the previous year and publicized a meeting with an advertising blitz. Before the initial meeting, a few of us got together with the faculty to work out our goals and organization, as well as to formulate a diagram articulating the role of the student group in the overall project. Our specific function was to work cooperatively with the director of the Academic Forum. The faculty seemed very excited that we were taking interest and initiative in our involvement with the program.

Fr. Kirby let us know that in the first few weeks of the semester Le Moyne College President O'Connell had sent a letter to all the student organizations and club presidents soliciting their support for the Values Program. The president asked the groups to schedule events specially relevant to economic justice, the year's theme. Our student group capitalized on this initiative by planning a component in our organization that would help coordinate publicity for the club events, and work with the head of the Academic Forum to plan the events calendar. It was the responsibility of this "networking committee" to build the coalitions among student organizations that proved to be so vital for our overall success. The key to motivating other student groups to use their resources for values-oriented events was due less to coercion than to sweeping them into our own group's enthusiasm. After working with Bruce Shefrin, the director of the Academic Forum, to contact the clubs initially, our success hinged on convincing them to jump on the bandwagon. We wanted to give fellow students the sense that their contribution would not only benefit their own group, but would also support this new effort of the college.

Another committee we devised was responsible for promoting and programming faculty-student functions, including panel debates, lectures, and dinner-discussions. The most important responsibility of this group was to maintain communications with the faculty, especially when events were coming up. Through this group, the collaborative structure of the project could continue to work effectively. The students working in this group enjoyed the closest contact with the faculty and helped the rest of us feel that we were working in a family atmosphere toward a common goal.

The third of the three committees included in the student group was responsible for programming our events, but I'll describe more about that later.

Another junior, Jill Greco, and I worked with the leaders of the three student committees to shape our goals and expectations. It's hard to describe the enthusiasm that we shared from the start. Our understanding that Le Moyne was breaking ground with this project generated much of our excitement, but our personal convictions and values inspired us as well. The student group strongly supported the efforts of the faculty, and we felt that, through our cooperation, we could have a great impact on the rest of the Le Moyne community. Little did we know how much resistance we would eventually encounter.

The first meeting, in the second week of September, attracted twenty-five students, mostly freshmen and sophomores. The number of underclassmen wasn't that surprising, since these younger students would be the ones to benefit from the project most. The prospect of being involved in this sort of program with the faculty was exciting for the younger students, especially when Fr. Kirby emphasized that the program could have implications beyond Le Moyne.

We separated into the committees that I described earlier and brainstormed a series of events that materialized later in the semester. The theme of economic justice was not especially inspiring until we began to learn about the variety and breadth of the topics it encompassed. A faculty member heard of the trouble we were having with generating ideas and responded, "Well, I think we've chosen the right topic then." I think, in retrospect, that she was right. We remained in a sort of limbo, high on enthusiasm and low on activity, until P.O.W.E.R., the minority group on campus, approached us with an idea.

Their organization was interested in planning events relating to apartheid in South Africa. Apparently, other minority groups in the area were doing similar work by bringing in speakers and planning awareness marches. This seemed to be the student group's opportunity to jump in and take some real steps toward action. We had had enough of the discussions concerning our goals and our plans; it was time to see what we could do. With P.O.W.E.R., we brainstormed a variety of different programs, lectures, movies, and activities that could bring the college community together to face a very serious problem in our world. The result was a full week of events, called "South Africa-Le Moyne." I suppose we won't get any award for the originality of the name, but that doesn't matter. And although the issue of apartheid did not engender debate, it did unite the community and draw an emotional response.

We considered ways that we could involve and inform a large part of the campus in a visible way. The idea of passing out armbands early in the week with an informational package about South Africa was adopted. By using armbands of two different colors, red and green, we separated the campus into an oppressed majority and a privileged minority. The campus was divided so that the reds could use only the back entrances to the buildings and inconvenient bathrooms. The reds were even segregated in the cafeteria and prohibited by the greens from having ice cream. Large signs proclaimed this segregation, and college officials—including the Residence Life staff were encouraged to enforce the restrictions. The means may seem to make light of a very serious issue, but there was no questioning the inequality that some students felt. After a few days of the simulation, the reds were even conspiring to revolt. The most effective part of this simulation came later in the week when we broke into classrooms and abducted students; we then "imprisoned" them in mock stockades located in the hallways of the academic buildings. With coverage from several television stations and newspapers, the event was as exciting as it was effective.

One of the other events that had a great influence on the impact of the week was a Donahue-style discussion, hosted by Barron Boyd, a professor of Political Science and an expert in South African politics. The discussion focused on the experiences of two South African students who attend Le Moyne. They recalled, for the audience, the many cruelties and injustices inflicted upon them and their families by the government. As one student told of her brother's abduction and the long trial of her family, she brought tears to the eyes of many in the audience. It struck me, then, that the most effective bridge in our values education stems from our emotional responses and from our instincts. We could be lectured at for hours about an issue taking place on the other side of the globe, but real emotional contact with that issue makes the most impact upon our values formation.

Other events included in the week were showings of the movies, *Biko*, and *Cry Freedom,* as well as a student-faculty dinner-discussion that focused on the economic situation in South Africa. It was our hope that through the variety and number of events offered, a large portion of the college community could be affected. From the amount of news coverage, we ended up reaching the larger community of Syracuse. It seemed to become clear to the rest of the college that our group was serious about our concern for issues, and about people suffering in a country half the world away.

The week ended with a dramatic and emotional march around the campus that Sunday evening. At least 150 students, faculty, and administrators participated, carrying banners, flags, and candles. Our march processed slowly around the campus, chanting and growing in number before we came to a fire prepared in the quad. To the tune of Peter Gabriel's, "Biko," the crowd burned all the armbands. The college president said a prayer for the end of all injustices and the end of racial tension at home and abroad. Looking at the faces around the fire, I felt that we had accomplished something significant. There is no way that such an event could have succeeded without the cooperation of student groups and collaboration with the faculty. The faculty was instrumental in supporting our program in the classrooms by encouraging involvement and publicizing events. The faculty group also helped us work through any snags we may have had with the administration.

We received no academic credit or stipend for our efforts, but that didn't matter. The satisfaction we felt in helping raise awareness of an issue of such importance was overwhelming. We had given people an opportunity to take a stand on an issue, and they took it. This was our first program, however, and one so large and complex was bound to have some problems. And, of course, student politics was involved. There was also no question that we had made a few mistakes along the way; several times there were breakdowns in communication and in the delegation of responsibilities. As peers trying to influence peers, we also seemed, to some, like a bunch of self-interested glory seekers. One group or another would complain about the lack of recognition, which was certainly unfortunate in light of our project goals. Though credit should go where it is due, recognition should not have been an expectation. There were plenty more lessons for us to learn along the way though.

A larger and more complex problem was that we had created a monster of sorts. Our first event was on such a grand scale that it would prove a difficult act to follow. The other problem was that South Africa-Le Moyne had required so much work that it left us exhausted for several weeks. How any of our student group kept up with schoolwork and other responsibilities is a very good question. Following South Africa-Le Moyne, most of the values events for the rest of the semester were coordinated by Dr. Bruce Shefrin, the director of the Academic Forum. Our student group lent its support with publicity, legwork, and attendance. Some of those events included a poetry reading dedicated to the year's theme, a multi-media production by the fine arts department that depicted poverty in paintings and sculpture, and a panel discussion run by the Honors Program.

At this time I was meeting with the faculty on a regular basis, contributing ideas, giving feedback, and keeping them informed of our activities. This close contact with the faculty was one of the most positive aspects of the project that our student group enjoyed, but it would be a matter of time before that closeness was also felt by the larger community. Later, this very positive, informal relationship would develop further through the student-faculty dinner-discussions sponsored through the Residence Life Office.

These dinner-discussions with students and faculty may prove to be a valuable part of the Academic Forum, if utilized. Not only are they effective in educating students about values issues through informal discussion, they also can strengthen the already close relationship between the faculty and the students. Our dinners were organized initially by the committee within our student group. Two or three faculty would be invited to lead discussions on particular issues with thirty to forty students. The first dinner-discussions to take place focused on organizational issues, on ways to bring values dialogue to the rest of the student body. Initially, the students in attendance were also members of the student group. But later in that first year, we were able to set up random invitations to attract students from other organizations in the college community. A dinner was planned for my all-male floor in the residence hall. The discussion topic was the issue of the environment in the future, and it prompted insightful dialogue as well as important questions. I was pleasantly surprised to see a floor of thirty-five freshmen show up (in ties), for a nice dinner and discussion that took almost two-and-a-half hours. Unfortunately, our contact was still somewhat restricted. It wasn't until the summer of 1989 that we devised a way for the rest of the residential students to be involved in these valuable discussions.

In the second semester, our student group spent most of its time working with Dr. Shefrin on the events that he had coordinated for the Forum. It was during that semester that the networking committee proved valuable for building coalitions among the various student organizations. These coalitions—a combination of the Industrial Relations Club, the Business Club, and the Political Science Academy, for example—would work together to plan a single event. Such a coalition was successful because of the cooperation between students and their faculty moderators. The events also were usually guaranteed an audience. As I mentioned before, when the networking committee was working up to its potential, it coordinated the specifics of the event and the publicity. The clubs themselves were responsible for paying for the events and integrating the year's theme.

The only big event that our student group planned on its own was an outdoor Spring Concert. The concert was sponsored by five college organizations and included four campus or local bands. Our plan was to have these bands play classic and contemporary music that focused on issues relating to war, drug abuse, racism, and government policy. With a minimal amount of money, we had ourselves a dramatic and fun event that 150-200 people enjoyed, despite some light rain. The root of the concert's success was the same for many of our events: a few people were captured by the idea that values issues were important and they invested themselves wholly in planning and implementation.

The concert capped off our student group's first year, and we felt very happy with what we had accomplished. One of the issues that faced us was the challenge of keeping the group intact until the next year. The larger problem we faced was how our group would involve more of the campus in the events. Luckily, most of the student group was young and very excited about the 1989-90 year.

In reviewing the successes of the past year, the most important features of the project had been the collaboration between students and faculty, and the ability that a few of us had to stir up the group's emotions on issues. These emotions insured inspiration and commitment to the projects that we undertook. Whenever that emotional commitment was lacking, so too was our interest in planning, or following through with, an event.

With the end of the 1989 spring semester, the faculty began their Summer Institute on peace and war. Again, students were not invited, and I believe that the program suffered during the 1989-90 year accordingly. It would be very valuable for the leaders of the student committee to have exposure to the same material and discussions as the Institute Fellows. This shared exposure would not only enhance our understanding of the issues at hand, but would also help to elucidate for us the somewhat complex structure of the Values Program.

During the summer, my last real contribution to the project was a package for the Student Life staff to use for the student-faculty dinner-discussions in the residence halls. The package included a list of values-related topics that were cross-referenced with the names of interested faculty members. All the resident advisers would have to do is contact these faculty, reserve a facility, contact the dining service, and publicize the event on their floor. I've found that good food is usually an incentive for students, but so is the prospect of meeting with faculty in an informal environment. The faculty were excited about the program; the only problem was that few of the resident advisors took advantage of the package this past year. My hope is that it will be used more often in the 1990-91 academic year.

As I took on the many challenges of senior year, I reduced my role in the 1989-90 Student Values Group to that of adviser. My successor, Alison Molea, will describe the course of our student program during 1989-90.

Another Student's Perspective

While the student Values Program ("Values" for short) has been a simultaneously fulfilling and chaotic dimension of my life for the past two years, the "why" and the "how" of my involvement can't be attributed to precise reasons. It began with a feeling, maybe of an obligation to serve, or a need to be a part of Le Moyne in an intimate, unique way. There are many organizations on campus centered around entertainment for students, existing solely for "fun." And while this is necessary and effective in promoting campus unity, I was attracted by the theme which Values seemed to promote—awareness.

Though it sounds odd, I joined Values during my sophomore year because of the name. I am not particularly a "label-conscious" buyer, but talk of an organization with "values" as the focus enticed me. It *sounded* challenging. I am amazed as I reflect today that though I had not acquired any information about Values, it still instantly drew me, and I now marvel at the depths of a challenge I had only heard of in passing.

I joined seeking involvement and wound up adding to my already over-extended extracurricular agenda. Over-involvement has always been a habit of mine, one which simultaneously fulfilled and worked against me throughout my education. I have always had a tendency, or even a need, to be *in medias res*. It could possibly be that I feel my life is whole only when my calendar is booked. This is not to say that Values is just another square to be penciled in. It has become significant in my life in a way no other clubs have been.

Assessing the impact of attending the first meeting, which David McCallum referred to in his essay, is a tough task. I did not plan to attend the meeting, but I remember walking by the classroom where it was held, peering in to see many raised hands and frustrated faces, and then opening the door. I was at a point in my life where I wanted to act and was interested in helping promote student awareness of important issues. I became involved because I was allowed to play a part in something which could reach many constituencies of the college community.

After the general success of South Africa-Le Moyne, in which other future committee members and I played minor roles in producing and distributing posters, I needed more. I wanted a deeper level of involvement, one that would allow me to make decisions and delegate authority. Other committee members similarly expressed a need for more significant roles. Thus, once praise of the event ceased, I became determined to be creatively productive the following semester, as far as promoting values issues was concerned.

A part of me was afraid that enthusiasm for Values would dissolve over the summer, so when students questioned me in September 1989 as to when Values was going to get started, I was both heartened and surprised. At the start of the semester, I asked David if seeking a higher position was feasible. Relieved that someone wanted to take charge of the project during his hectic senior year, David encouraged me wholeheartedly. Jim Garvin, a student and friend with whom I had worked closely the previous semester, also shared my enthusiasm, and we became self-appointed co-chairpersons, with David's consent.

I remember feeling elated that I had a position with such potential. I would be partly responsible for creating an addition to the community that the faculty and other segments of the college deemed extremely important. Actually, this realization was rather overwhelming, but it was what I needed to get going.

Our first task was to have Values recognized as a club on campus, so that money could be allotted. We were told we had to propose our purposes and goals to the college's Student Senate board, to be voted on as to their worthiness. So we called a meeting. "Calling meetings" became an omnipresent part of my vocabulary. Whenever there was conflict, or questions, or a need to inform, we called meetings—at least once a week. It got to the point where I set aside time for a Values meeting every week for a month, only I did it in October, looking ahead to November! I found that in order to be correctly organized, I would have to allot a block of time in my schedule for Values work. I soon realized that working on the Values committee could be a full-time job.

At this gathering of committee heads, we tried to come up with a motto. Up until this point, we simply *knew* we wanted to do this Values "stuff," but having to be recognized by the senate made us put these thoughts into words. I see this verbalizing process as the most significant aspect of the fall semester because it forced us to define our goals and ideals. It enabled us to get perspective, to make Values more tangible. Before this meeting, when asked what Values was, many of us would respond by referring first to South Africa-Le Moyne as an example of what Values supported and was capable of carrying out. This helped others to get a broad sense of what we stood for. If they knew we supported "this type" of event, they would understand.

But it certainly wasn't enough. We needed a foundation to draw from because without the "right behind our might" we would have floundered. At the same time, we felt we should change the name, because we thought "Values" was too vague, too "administration-like." We desired our own name, one that would embody all we stood for. So the seven of us wound up in a contest, attempting to come up with an appropriate acronym with each letter representing a different characteristic of Values. A popular acronym was "AWARE," which stood for "Always Wanting to Arouse Real Enlightenment." After much laughter at the contest results, we decided to keep the "Values" name and construct a solid statement of purpose. "To enlighten and to engender a spirit of awareness" became our battle cry. We proposed this to the senate and were approved. We were finally official!

A general meeting was scheduled, and none of us expected thirty-five people to attend! Pleased with the turnout and relieved at the interest, we came to believe that Values was going places. The students wanted it—what more could we ask for? Another asset was the faculty-staff turnout. Several hall directors and teachers showed up and participated, providing encouragement and approval. Their presence helped Jim and me look professional, despite the nervous tension that was the source of our energy that night. We asked all who were interested in holding a position on Values to submit an essay stating their motivation for joining. We wanted a deeply motivated committee which manifested an interest in values, and an essay could be a means for the applicants to assess their motivations. The resulting essays were few but qualified—we received exactly enough applicants for our committee positions. The pieces were falling into place.

We designated positions on the committee according to the previous semester's organization of Values. A networking chairperson would work through other clubs and organizations on campus for funding, publicity, and brainstorming. A publicity director was established, along with two programming directors who would be the main centers for feedback and action. And we designated a chairperson to be the faculty-student liaison, an intricate part of the Values Committee's success.

I was interested to know the committee members' feelings and ideas about Values—and their essays provided a good overview of their perspectives. Catherine Ward, networking chair, stated that she had much to offer the Values committee because she "believed in the Le Moyne community." She stressed that Le Moyne had many "natural resources" that could be tapped and put to use. She wanted Values to promote a sense of community and believed that our success would come with group effort. Our publishing director, Rhonda Balzano, who had much experience in communications, applied because she felt able to inform others about issues and happenings in a creative manner. Erik Sudigala and Mary Beth Brennan, the programming directors, both sought a deeper involvement. Mary Beth wrote: "I cannot count the number of times I have said 'I wish I could help' or 'I want to be able to make a difference.' I feel, though, that I could do both through the Values committee." Erik had worked on Values the semester before and wanted a stronger role with more responsibility. He looked forward to dealing with people and promoting enthusiasm. Brian Heffern, faculty-student chair, felt he could do a respectable job working with the faculty. Familiar with professors with whom we would have frequent contact, he was confident that he could act as a "contact person" consistently and professionally.

So with a determination to revise the community (and the world, I think), we held our first official meeting, sending out notices and posting signs. And all this was done on our own initiative. The signs read, "Where Are Your Values?" and "Values meeting—Do you have any?" in the hope that the questions would be humorous and captivating enough to stir interest. Good publicity would be perfect bait for the interested mind.

Once again Jim and I found ourselves anxious about attendance. And this time rightly so. When you've scheduled an 8 p.m. meeting on a Monday night and you suddenly remember about Monday night football, panic sets in. Still, it was surprisingly well attended. We opened the meeting by expressing our interest and enthusiasm for what we wanted to accomplish. Jim and I felt that announcing our motivations (and even our fears) would encourage others to offer suggestions and provide criticism. We stressed that at all times we wanted to hear their opinions.

In the second half of the meeting, the brainstorming began. We kept in the forefront the fact that "Peace and War" was the designated issue. The committee heads had previously decided we would devote one week in the fall to "War" and another in the spring to "Peace," believing that a concentrated week of Values events would have the greatest impact and would avoid our having to reserve dates and rooms sporadically from September to December. In response to a call for suggestions about how to structure the week, hands shot up. A movie festival was suggested, featuring *Platoon* and other films on the Vietnam War. Someone proposed a lecture series on the effects of atomic war, concluding with the movie, *The Day After*. They wanted a concert, the music reverberating Springsteen's question, "War— What Is it Good For?" And all sought to be creative, to approach the issue from a unique angle that would attract the necessary attention and make students realize the depth of our concern for the issue.

Overall, this enthusiasm was heartening. We left the meeting on an "involvement high," rather dazed at what we had the potential to accomplish. Another "gem" from this meeting was the realization that we had resources, as Catherine mentioned in her essay. We had a newspaper, a radio station, and a supportive faculty at our disposal. These, if used, would make our desire to communicate Values simpler, more "worldwide." Jim and I, and the rest of the committee, were elated at our prospects. We would be "doing" Values.

After the meeting, all of us had specific jobs to carry out. Some were to talk to teachers, some were to reserve rooms, still others were to recruit support from other clubs for "Values Week '89." We arranged lectures, anticipating a maximum of thirty attendees. We showed the movie, *The Day After,* with discussion afterward. In memory of POWs from the upstate area, a list of names was posted outside the chapel. A student-faculty dinner-discussion was held, and "Splatball," a simulated war game with paint pellets and plastic guns, was played on the last day of the week, with a dinner-discussion held afterwards. The student newspaper, *The Dolphin,* provided articles about our goals, the radio station announced events, and we posted signs, listing a schedule of activities.

But unfortunately, a speaker's name was misspelled on posters. We had financially supported another club which had arranged for him to speak at Le Moyne. Until the day of his arrival, we had not been aware of our error. Somewhere along the way a detail had been overlooked—but it was an important detail. We had embarrassed other clubs and looked extremely unprofessional. And it didn't end there.

The event we were most proud of scheduling was Splatball, which we felt would be an appropriate means of experiencing war, even though you "guard your life" with only toys and paint. Buses were reserved, as the game was played in a vast wooded area situated about an hour from school. But who had remembered that the bus driver was to be paid in advance? The committee member responsible for the reservations had assumed that bills could be sent and paid afterwards (but we all know what happens when we assume). Luckily, due to the generosity of the bus company and the Splatball organizers, we were billed later. It was a very close call.

Though an extremely stimulating experience, as the participants in the follow-up dinner-discussion attested, Splatball drained our funds. Jim and I knew that refills of paint pellets for the guns would cost extra money but didn't realize that the money was not to be had. We should have kept a tab, should have looked into a million small details beforehand. In addition to "call a meeting," "should have" became another oft-repeated phrase that semester. And it was a defeating feeling, getting off the bus from a successful Splatball event with forty-five fatigued (literally) and paint-splattered students, realizing that financial mistakes and spelling errors had worked against us during our "War Week '89." We wondered what the community was going to think.

We found out promptly by reading the editorial section of our campus newspaper. In it the Values Committee was accused of being unprofessional and threatening. We were told that we tried to come across as elitist and righteous by posting signs asking "Where Are Your Values?" The author noted that attendance of the week's events had been low even though the committee was boasting about its success.

How do we go about enticing our peers into enlightenment about topics without appearing to know more than they do? The signs stating "Where Are Your Values?" had been meant as a challenge, encouraging others to attend a meeting and to reflect on their own situations. Instead, people took the signs to say that we had more information, had "superior values." Yes, we felt gravely misunderstood, and today this issue still stands. Probably the main reason that Values had been so slow in starting again the following semester was this "peer factor."

Yet to say we failed is wrong; despite our shortcomings, the committee felt fulfilled in many ways. As mentioned, one of the events of the week had been a faculty-student dinner-discussion on the subject, "Is War Ever Justified?" This event counteracted the heavy feelings of defeat we all had experienced; it was a prime example of what Values should model. Committee members, resident advisors, and select faculty whom the committee felt could contribute provocative opinions on the topic were asked to participate. The result was unexpectedly sensational.

The seating was designed for a one-to-five ratio of faculty to students at each table. The faculty as well as the students represented a variety of disciplines; one of our greatest assets was the diversity in the room. After dinner, Jim and I initiated discussion by introducing two professors who had been asked beforehand to prepare and present opinions for and against war. When they proposed their views, a heated debate arose as participants became adamant in supporting a side.

Afterwards, Jim and I just smiled at one another because we knew that we really had helped engender "a spirit of awareness" on campus. Talking afterwards, we agreed that the past problems were insignificant because now we had organized students and faculty; we were discussing a vital values issue. People left the dinner more aware of their stands, possibly even angered at others for their beliefs. The dinner centered on the arms race, the church's view of just war, pacifism, and related issues. To sit and *discuss* and watch others defend the pros and cons of war and the emotions connected with their views was fascinating. It made us feel whole and accomplished.

Another consolation was our realization that the semester had been an experiment. Eager to see results and spurred by Student Senate recognition, we attempted to run towards our goals with blinders on. We had no warnings or guidelines or specific models to work from. In short, at the end of the fall semester, it was comforting to know we had a second chance, another semester during which we could carry out proposals.

In looking to the future, one area I'd like to see strengthened is faculty-student communications. Though our entire committee is comprised of student leaders who hold key positions in high school and college organizations, we need support. We need to sharpen our ties with faculty, utilize them as a resource, let them know we want their input and ideas on events we decide to program. This support would help us overcome the "peer factor" because it would enable the student body to see that "Values Talk" is not restricted to a club; it should extend to all areas of Le Moyne life. Values should be a part of any event which proposes to expand one's awareness of a topic—it should be a tool of enlightenment.

Though the student Values committee shares the faculty's outlook, the problem lies in getting other students to agree. Students should be responsible for broadening the horizons of their peers. What scares me is that in attempting to do so, I am criticized by those who, for whatever reason, do not have the desire or the energy to allow their perspectives to be expanded to include neglected issues of the world or, on a smaller scale, the surrounding community.

So the middle of March is upon me, Spring Break '90 only forty-eight hours away, and the student Values committee has not yet programmed a single event. I attribute this to my heavy schedule, but more so to my fear of the negative reactions I *may* encounter if all does not go perfectly. I am hesitant to fail.

An extremely wise person in my life inscribed this insight in a book she once gave me: "Experience is the hardest teacher because she gives the test first, the lesson afterwards." This quote forced the full weight of its meaning on my consciousness at the end of "War Week '89." The hard work and disappointments were worth the effort, as our errors showed us the difficulties involved with transforming ideal visions into real and effective programs for our peers. We learned we have the power to spark feelings on significant, worldly issues, and this has been the greatest value we experienced.

Part Three: Assessment

8

The Struggle for Institutional Support

The Deadline

It was 2:00 p.m. on a rainy October afternoon in 1987 when Donald Kirby, Values Program director and faculty colleague in religious studies, knocked anxiously on my office door.

"We've got a problem."

"No! Not now. The deadline's at four o'clock today if we are going to get the application in the mail on time," I replied.

"I know, but the President won't sign the cover sheet without the Academic Dean's approval. And the Dean won't sign because the Treasurer and the Development Officer won't approve the application. I don't know what we're going to do," said Don.

"What's the problem with Development and the Treasurer? I thought we had been over all that."

"The Development Office doesn't like being committed to raising matching funds, and the Treasurer thinks we overlooked hidden overhead costs. At least, that's what the Dean just told me on the phone. I can't get through to Development."

"Why don't we get some other [Values] Group members involved?" I suggested. "John [Langdon] has dealt with Development before, and Bruce [Shefrin] has gone over the numbers with the Treasurer. If they can iron out the problems, I could go with you to ask for the Dean's and President's approval."

"OK, but we've got to move quickly. I can't believe this is happening so late in the game." Don was annoyed and stressed at the same time.

Ever since the Values Group had been asked to draw up a grant proposal for the Consortium for the Advancement of Higher Education (CAPHE) six weeks earlier, we had worked under pressure. In the first place, none of us had ever written this sort of grant proposal, and it quickly became clear that the Development Office had insufficient experience in working with faculty. Second, members of the Values Group had not yet reached agreement about how to promote values education at the college. Even our vocabulary regarding values education was in flux. Finally, we wanted to make our first major proposal especially strong, since it would likely set the tone for subsequent proposals and for our relationships with other prospective funding agencies. With some much-needed outside help, we had worked hard—only to run into these last-minute administrative snags.

To be sure, this story did end happily. The key administrators, after some complaining about being rushed, gave their approval, and we met the grant application deadline. Some months later, we were notified that the proposal was successful. Still, gaining final approval for the grant proposal need not have been such a struggle. Although none of the Values Group members were politically inexperienced, we learned some important lessons about building institutional, administrative, and financial support.

Building Administrative Support

Founded in 1947, Le Moyne College has a strong commitment to providing its nearly 1,900 students with a liberal arts education in the Jesuit tradition. Its small endowment renders it dependent upon student tuition for most of its operating budget. Efforts to change this situation by raising funds have met with limited success. As in many similar colleges, faculty have not sought outside grants for institutional projects for the usual reasons, including a heavy teaching load (seven courses per academic year), too few faculty in same subdisciplines, and lack of adequate support facilities. For these reasons and others, the college lacks experience in raising outside funds for directly academic or educational projects.

Early on, the Values Group recognized that it would have to raise money from outside sources for the Values Program alone. Some members of the committee had experience in applying for individual research grants, but none had applied for any institutional grants. For that, we knew we would need help. To our knowledge, we were the first faculty group to approach the college's Development Office for assistance in locating prospective funding agencies and in developing proposals.

In addition, many institutions in higher education in the United States must raise funds for buildings already built or in progress. Resources devoted to such tasks leave little staff time and energy for supporting untested projects, especially in the "soft" academic areas. It sometimes seems as if institutional priorities become skewed. Because Le Moyne College is typical in this regard, it is not surprising that conflicts arise over what people perceive their institutional roles to be.

Beyond giving us a copy of the *Foundation Directory,* the chief development officer, concerned that his office might be distracted from more important tasks, was disinclined to help. During a meeting convened to resolve our differences, this administrator told us that he feared our fund-raising efforts might impede or compete with his own. Moreover, the assistant development officer charged with general responsibility for assisting faculty was too busy with other tasks to be of much help at first, though he proved invaluable later on. In any event we found that we were essentially on our own as an untried committee proposing a novel approach to the unconsidered problem of values education.

Other administrators also regarded our venture suspiciously. We were not, after all, part of the normal administrative or faculty senate bureaucracy. Were we trying to appropriate the moral identity of the institution? Were we religious or ethical fanatics whose harebrained schemes could harm the public image of the college? Were we likely to encroach on administrative decision-making or on legitimate faculty responsibilities?

Would we end up costing the college money by requiring support from the already tight operating budget or by generating hidden costs in terms of overhead? Would we, in sum, be more trouble than we were worth? Pointing out that such questions might be raised legitimately, at least by others, the academic dean directly informed us at an initial meeting in 1986 that no substantial funds for the project would be contributed by the college. If we were to go forward, we would have to convince outside funding agencies that our project was worth supporting. He told us, moreover, that he expected to be kept apprised of what we were doing to make sure that we did not contradict the mission of the college or prematurely commit the institution to a program beyond its resources.

Without detailing the history of our triumphs and defeats, I shall delineate what we have learned thus far about gaining legitimacy in the eyes of administrators for a project such as the Values Program at Le Moyne College. Although none of these recommendations is original, we found them all too easy to overlook. We learned that we had to work hard and use effective strategies to have our program recognized as a contribution to the college worthy of support.

1. *Keep administrators informed.* Initially supported by a small grant from the Raskob Foundation, we began as an ad hoc discussion group entirely outside the normal bureaucratic structure of the institution. The principal advantage to our having no institutional standing was the degree of freedom in discussing various problems and possible solutions pertaining to values education. We were able to function as a interdisciplinary group focused on a particular problem. During the first year, we became convinced that some sort of action was needed to improve the ethical dimension of our students' education; it also was clear from our discussions that a doctrinaire approach would be out of the question.

   In order to keep administrative concerns in view, we invited one administrator (the director of admissions, selected primarily because of his knowledge of our students' backgrounds) into the group. Thus, informally and within the group, a channel of communication was intentionally maintained. We also informed the academic dean of our existence and assured him that we would report any significant results of our discussions to him. Since the president and Don Kirby had worked together to obtain the initial Raskob grant, the president took an early interest in the group's activities. However cautious the senior administrators remained during the early stages, keeping them well informed was vital to gaining their support.

2. *Select well-respected, experienced persons for the initial group.* There is no way to appear modest in expressing this point, but the point is crucial. If the group has no official standing, its efforts will be given a respectful hearing only to the extent that its members are already respected. Our initial group of seven people, for example, was composed of the college's director of admissions and six tenured faculty members, including four current or recent department chairs, several current or recent officers or committee chairs of the Faculty Senate, one Jesuit who had previously chaired a Values Audit at Le Moyne, and representatives of various disciplines in the humanities and the social sciences. Because of their previous service to the institution, Values Group members were seen as having the best interests of the college at heart.

3. *Think like an administrator.* Administrators, rightly, tend to be cautious in approving new ventures. After all, there is usually keen competition for always limited resources. New ventures frequently utilize more resources than originally planned, and they often develop a momentum of their own that leads them to consume even more resources. Administrators must be confident that a new venture will promote their institution's central educational mission.

Although we were somewhat prepared for the academic dean's reluctance to commit college funds to our project, we were inexperienced in the ways of a college development office. Because Le Moyne's Development Office typically did not work with faculty in seeking outside funding for any project, we expected resistance to requests for direct assistance to our group. When our initial requests for assistance were rebuffed, we doggedly repeated those requests even as we undertook our own fund-raising efforts. (Our persistence did provide the occasion for an assistant development officer to become so committed to the project that he devoted a great deal of his personal time to helping us!) We were unprepared, however, for the chief development officer's view that our fund-raising efforts were in competition with other fund-raising activity conducted by his office.

In our case, the president's early interest and support led him to overrule the chief development officer's objections to applying for the matching grant from CAPHE. The president also agreed that in this instance our fundraising efforts would not encroach on college campaigns already under way or contemplated. Although we were never able to resolve the conflict with the chief development officer directly, appealing to a more senior administrator resolved the conflict over institutional roles.

Despite our experience with administrators on matters essentially internal to the institution, we initially overlooked the extent to which senior administrators must consider other constituencies external to the college. We eventually learned that once these administrators were convinced of the desirability of the Values Program, the program became a staple in their public utterances. The president, for example, frequently praised the program in addresses to the trustees and regents of the college even before any significant activity had occurred. The public relations value of the program was something of a surprise to us and could have been used more to the program's advantage, especially insofar as administrators themselves continued to promote the program publicly while withholding internal financial support. Had we come to an early mutual understanding with administrators concerning the Values Program's usefulness in expressing the educational mission of the college, we would have been in a much stronger position when arguing for adequate support services and resources.

4. *Request administrative assistance as necessary.* While we did not always receive the resources that we sought, we persisted in requesting various sorts of assistance: financial, secretarial, budget writing, proposal drafting, etc. For example, we found while drafting the CAPHE proposal that the college lacked expertise in drafting grant proposals for academic ventures. We persisted in requesting guidance until we secured outside help. Such assistance made the difference. When the assistant development officer who had been so helpful moved to another institution, we pressed the academic dean and the president hard for a highly qualified replacement—with eventual success.

A group can also request other assistance from administrators that will actually help build administrative support for the project. For instance, when our first grant proposal drafts had reached a relatively mature stage in terms of the Values Group's thinking, we asked the academic dean and, later, the president, to offer their editorial advice. We held several meetings, especially with the dean, to clarify certain features of the drafts. Administrative editing at the highest possible level is important because it provides an opportunity to sell the project to administrators and to allow them to see that the project is in line with their own thinking about the mission of the institution. We also found that administrators become supportive of proposals to which they contribute.

Presidential support for the program has proved enormously important, especially on campus. The president, for instance, sent a letter to various organizations, asking that their college activities, clubs, and events be coordinated around the theme established each year for the Values Program. Thus, during the first year, several activities and events centered on the theme of economic justice. Only such highly visible administrative support and public action could have accomplished that result.

Given the Values Group's eventual success in building administrative support, how can we understand the snags that developed in the story recounted at the beginning of this chapter? The problems that occurred on that October afternoon were not ideological. By that point in the process, both the academic dean and the president had approved of the idea of a Values Program. The primary problem lay in an unresolved conflict concerning the expectations of the Values Group and those of the Development Office. The Values Group expected the Development Office to assist the committee in its fund-raising efforts and to raise matching funds if necessary. The Development Office, however, expected the Values Group not to interfere with development efforts already under way. (The problem with the treasurer was primarily one of miscommunication.)

Although it has taken over three years, we now seem to have resolved the conflict concerning fund-raising efforts. Because of the Values Group's persistent requests, as well as other faculty and administrative needs, the college has recently secured the services of a highly qualified person to coordinate submission of grant proposals by the faculty. This official, who holds a Ph.D. in the social sciences and who has extensive teaching and fund-raising experience, is able to communicate with the faculty and to assist in designing the program in a way that is more attractive to potential sources of financial support. With his guidance, the Values Program continues to obtain funding for its activities. Other individuals and groups from the faculty are also able to move forward with their own proposals as a result. Indeed, the current level of good service from the Development Office is probably anomalous for institutions of our type, and it has helped Le Moyne to overcome the faculty versus development rifts that appear to be pandemic in higher education.

Building Financial Support

As the preceding discussion indicates, strong administrative support is vital for putting a values program on a sound financial footing. The Values Program at Le Moyne continues to thrive on the basis of a combination of external funding and a modest allocation of internal funds from college resources. Although the program continues to raise outside funds with the help of the Development Office, not all of our efforts have proved fruitful. From our moderately successful experience we have learned several lessons.

1. *Seek advice from the staff of prospective funding sources, remembering that such assistance can be ambiguous.* During the years 1986-88, much time and effort was devoted to submitting and then resubmitting a major proposal for funding the Summer Institutes and the Academic Forum. Although these two efforts ultimately failed, they were highly instructive.

   The successful CAPHE proposal had already taught us the value of expert assistance in writing proposals. We therefore retained the same two outside consultants for the subsequent effort. In addition, we made contact fairly early with an officer of the prospective funding agency to help shape and refine the proposal.

   Despite the officer's many helpful suggestions, we soon found ourselves in something of a tug of war over how we wished to conceive and describe our program and the sort of proposal the agency was willing to fund. As explained elsewhere, we wished to emphasize "values education" and to implement a broad program affecting classroom teaching and student extracurricular experience, whereas the funding agency wished to support a more traditional approach, including visible curricular changes in terms of new courses. Although these differences were artfully papered over by ambiguities of language, in the end they were not negotiated artfully enough. Language is not infinitely malleable, and the question of how far we were willing to go to mold our program according to the agency's ideological agenda proved difficult. In this instance, failure to be funded was helpful: had our proposal been funded, the program might have gone in a direction that we did not desire.

   Encouraged by the funding agency, we resubmitted a year later. This time we dealt with a different agency officer whose advice turned out to be misleading. Although we responded positively to the officer's every suggestion in the revised draft, the fundamental tension between our objectives and the agency's objectives actually increased. We should have been alert enough to notice the widening gap, but, relying too much on the assurances of the agency officer, we did not. A prospective funding agency's advice must, of course, be heeded; but we discovered that it helps to check that advice against the experience of others who have already dealt successfully with a particular agency.

2. *Remember that successful proposals generate further success.* The initial planning stages of the Le Moyne Values Program were supported by a series of grants from the Raskob Foundation. Their approval of our second proposal surprised us because our first year of planning had led us in directions not envisioned in our first Raskob proposal. Our goals, however, coincided with Raskob's, and they have continued to support the program with additional grants. Similarly, substantial support from an anonymous foundation was renewed upon the successful completion of the program's first year. And finally, CAPHE's positive experience of our program contributed to their decision to support an unrelated Le Moyne College program which is directed toward recruiting local secondary school students into the teaching profession.

External funding agencies frequently come to have a stake in the projects they support. Provided that such projects can demonstrate an adequate degree of success, funding agencies often seek to build upon their initial investment and to extend their relationship with the host institution. Project committees and development officers should pursue this advantage.

3. *Establish an adequate research and evaluation component early in the project.* Having such procedures in place simplifies writing grant proposals. The nature of the evaluation to be carried out can actually affect the shape of some aspects of a program, especially with

regard to how its objectives are formulated. In addition, since funding agencies understandably require regular reports on how effectively funds are used, it helps to have an evaluation procedure in place. A grant proposal can then explain the evaluation procedure without having to fashion a new or different procedure for each prospective funding agency.

The Le Moyne College Values Program has appropriate evaluation procedures which have already generated significant conclusions and recommendations about various aspects of the program. (See chapter 9 on research and evaluation.) Moreover, as we seek to expand the Values Program, an expansion of research and evaluation efforts is also required. In early 1990, the Lilly Endowment awarded us a substantial grant to support our further development of these efforts.

4. *Seek permanent funding as soon as possible.* The Values Group has just begun this phase of its fund-raising efforts. Academic administrators of the college are now convinced that the program deserves internal budgetary support. Incorporating some financial aid for the Values Program into the institutional budgeting structure of the college demonstrates to others the college's commitment to the program.

The college lacks the resources, however, to support the program fully out of the operational budget. Therefore, it is necessary to continue to seek outside funds sufficient to endow substantial portions of the program or to support the program on a continuing basis. This is a difficult challenge, though we hope not insurmountable, insofar as prospective funding sources frequently prefer to support new rather than established programs. Receiving funding for an established program, however successful the program might be, can turn out to be more difficult than funding an innovative, untested program.

Building Faculty Support

Even as the Values Group worked at securing administrative support, we began to worry about the reaction of our faculty colleagues. The college's historic concern for values in education, the recently completed Values Audit, and general faculty complaints about "careerism" among students, as well as other factors, predisposed the faculty to be receptive to some initiative. And the Values Group was well "plugged in" to the faculty, both formally and informally. But we feared our colleagues could misunderstand our approach as elitist or dogmatic. "Values," after all, is a loaded term in American higher education. As a result of our experience, we offer the following guidelines.

1. *Communicate the objectives of the program in a nonthreatening way.* College and university faculty are hardly of one mind regarding values education. Many believe that values considerations cannot or should not be introduced into classroom discussions either because of a fear of indoctrination or because of adherence to an ideal of "objective," scientific inquiry. Such views are widely held not only by natural and social scientists, but also by humanities faculty who equate rigorous scholarship with "value-free" inquiry. A significant number of faculty at Le Moyne therefore might have been expected to regard values education as floundering in the swamp of unfounded personal opinion or subjective aesthetic taste. Interestingly, although plans for the Values Program have been public knowledge and the Program has now been implemented for at least two years, few such objections have been raised. We believe that this lack of opposition at Le Moyne is due to the college's Jesuit heritage, the faculty's long-standing commitment to a significant core curriculum, some self-selection among those faculty who choose to teach at Le Moyne, and the convincing argument for values in education, among other factors. Other institutions, however, will need to approach this concern from their own unique contexts.

Despite a lack of strong faculty opposition at Le Moyne, we had to be careful with the design of the program and in our communications with the faculty. If the program were perceived as aiming at religious indoctrination or as proceeding from moral elitism, it would be quickly doomed. Such considerations played an explicit role in the planning stages, for we realized that the faculty was much more heterogeneous than the student body in terms of background. In all of our contacts with the faculty about the program, we had to be uniformly clear that we used the term "values education" in a particular way—a way that might overlap, but did not coincide, with its common usage. While we were prepared to argue for the scholarly legitimacy of considering values in the context of all academic disciplines, we always stressed the *educational* benefits of the program. That is, the program would help students recognize values issues, understand values positions, and reach some critical judgment about what they had just analyzed. We were very clear that, while the educational process itself presupposes a general values orientation relating to what is necessary for academic inquiry and exchange, we were not interested in "pushing" only one set of values to be accepted by our students.

After extensive discussion within the Values Group to reach agreement on a common approach to values education, we employed two strategies to allay potential faculty fears. First, during informal conversations with colleagues and in written explanations of the first Summer Institute, we stressed the intellectual content and focus of the program. Our invitation to faculty to apply for the Summer Institute described the sort of intellectual discussion that we envisioned and emphasized our expectation that each participant would be committed to changes in course content or in teaching methods. Second, as a foretaste of the serious intellectual nature of the Values Program, we invited Dr. Richard Morrill, one of the first Institute's facilitators, to give a keynote address in the spring of 1988 preceding the first Summer Institute. In all, our aim was to show that the Values Program was not an exercise in subjective "values clarification" but an educational effort that would respect the pluralism of the college community.

2. *Take bureaucratic and political realities into account.* In addition to these philosophical issues, we also had to consider bureaucratic and political sensibilities. Since the Values Group and the Values Program never enjoyed any official bureaucratic standing, we could easily have been perceived as trying to circumvent established procedures and structures. Moreover, insofar as the program impinged upon the curriculum, the Values Group might be misunderstood as trying to usurp some of the responsibilities of the Curriculum Committee and the Faculty Senate. There was also the possibility that aspects of the program might, unintentionally, duplicate others' efforts in their own departments. Finally, some colleagues might object to any use of college funds or resources to support the Values Program when other needs were going unmet.

Our basic approach to these bureaucratic considerations was informal. Members of the Values Group sat on the Curriculum Committee and on the Executive Board of the Faculty Senate and were, therefore, in a position to keep these bodies fully informed of our intentions and activities. We abided by normal procedures as established by the Faculty Senate. We also tried to make certain that everyone understood that all financial support for the initial planning and implementation of the program (except for any faculty time volunteered) was to come from outside sources. By announcing the first Summer Institute in the context of announcing the CAPHE grant to support it, we were able to demonstrate that the Values Program was recognized by prestigious outside funding sources and so would depend primarily on external funds for its operation.

3. *Build support by enlisting help in implementation.* In order to prevent misunderstanding and ensure maxi-

mum faculty participation in the Values Program, we pursued three avenues of communication. First, as mentioned above, the original committee was very careful to keep relevant committees of the Faculty Senate fully informed about all actions taken to implement the program. Second, shortly after moving to the stage of applying for outside funding and initiating steps toward implementation, we expanded the membership of the committee to include faculty from other disciplines as well as additional administrators. Third, our invitation to the faculty to participate in the first Summer Institute provided a good occasion to explain the Values Program in some detail.

Keeping the various faculty committees informed was crucial to preventing misunderstanding. For instance, some of our funding applications mentioned the curricular impact of the program, and it was true that we intended to influence the classroom experience of Le Moyne students across most disciplines. But since the faculty had just completed a six-year, sometimes bruising revision of the core curriculum, we felt compelled to reassure the Faculty Senate that we intended no revision of the curriculum in terms of developing new courses or requirements. We repeated such reassurances whenever necessary. At the same time, we made clear our hope that individual faculty members might revise some of their courses as a result of the program, but that such revisions, we were sure, could be handled in the normal course of faculty business.

Expansion of the original Values Group became necessary as soon as we moved into the fund-raising and implementation stage of the program. Initially, we were unsuccessful in recruiting a faculty representative from literature because of the amount of time that such committee service would require, but we did secure the participation of faculty members from philosophy and mathematics along with the participation of the assistant academic dean (because of his administrative expertise and knowledge of minority affairs) and the director of counseling services (because of her direct experience of students' lives outside the classroom). Enlisting the participation of social science faculty to carry out research and evaluation and to assist in planning the program proved crucial later on. In addition, through an enlarging network of subcommittees to plan the Summer Institutes, the Academic Forum, and research/evaluation, a larger number of faculty soon became familiar with the details of the program and to become committed to it. Merely organizing all this activity, in addition to writing funding proposals, soon became the major task of the expanded Values Group.

Ultimately, implementation of the Values Program became the most important means of building faculty support. At a formal convocation of the faculty in January 1988, the president of the College announced that the theme for the first year's Summer Institute and Academic Forum would be economic justice. The president on that occasion (and subsequently) warmly endorsed the program and urged the Le Moyne community to support it. Formal presentations were also made to the Executive Board of the Faculty Senate and to a meeting of department chairs. Further explanations of the program occurred when faculty were invited to submit applications to participate in the first Summer Institute. This process was repeated for the second Summer Institute. As explained in the conclusion to this book, the success of the Summer Institutes has been the most important factor in building strong faculty support. The activities of the Academic Forum, in which many faculty participated directly, also generated faculty support.

Although building faculty support for the Values Program did not prove especially difficult, given the institutional history and ethos of Le Moyne College, some care had to be taken to avoid misunderstanding and bureaucratic conflict. Having a committee composed of both faculty and administrators, expanding the committee by inviting faculty to participate in planning and implementing the program (thereby changing the program in useful ways), keeping official bodies informed of the program's progress, and using the program itself as a means for increasing faculty support all proved to be important factors in ensuring the program's success.

Building Student Support

Quite frankly, the task of building student support for the Values Program struck us all as a daunting mystery. After all, student apathy in general, a nearly universal lack of concern for social values, and student ignorance about the world and its problems were all major reasons for the program in the first place! To be sure, a small minority of students were concerned about matters other than their own careers, and we could therefore count on some support. But we worried about how to reach the larger number of students who seemed complacent in their careerist individualism. Of course, classroom aspects of the program could be initiated by the faculty unilaterally. But student participation in the Academic Forum—lectures, symposia, films, dramatic productions, etc.—was by no means assured. Our suggestions for building student support follow.

1. *Recruit administrators who work with students to join the committee.* Having the director of counseling services and the assistant academic dean for minority affairs join the Values Group early in the first year of implementation helped immensely. Some of the committee members had little first-hand knowledge of how we might go about enlisting student participation, but these two administrators were much more experienced. Their insights, derived from their direct experience with students on campus, helped to shape certain details of the program. Moreover, at their suggestion, we soon began to plan formal presentations to various student committees and organizations. But the most important development in building student support began initially as a setback.

2. *Invite students to help plan and fund major parts of the program.* In planning for the Academic Forum, the Values Group had devised an ambitious list of lectures and symposia involving participation by several nation-

ally recognized experts. It was a truly dazzling list—
and dazzlingly expensive! As it turned out, we were unable to raise the funds necessary to support these activities. This inability to raise the necessary funds for
the Academic Forum as planned forced us, as one committee member put it later, into the "necessity of going
out and beating up on club presidents and department
chairs and students and organizations on the campus" to
get them to support the program. And that resulted,
again in the committee member's words, "in their
buying into the project rather than being bought by the
project."

Communication with student groups—the Student
Senate and various student academic or social service
organizations—was not easy. Values Group members
with ties to the Student Life Office arranged for other
committee members to make formal presentations at
meetings of student organizations. Our chief concern
was to emphasize how students might contribute to the
planning of activities relevant to the Values Program
and how the Values Program might assist students with
their organization's program. We felt, correctly as it
turned out, that the question of money would be
resolved once the students' participation was secured.

In these circumstances, the lack of funds forced us to
ask for organizational and financial support from
various student clubs and committees. This meant that
a fairly representative group of students became directly
involved in the planning of Academic Forum events.
After all, it would make no sense to them to provide
money for a project in which they had no meaningful
planning role. In several instances, students who had
been involved in or witnessed the struggle for economic
justice in poorer areas of the city or in other countries
produced programs for the Academic Forum. Others
took a leading role in planning and carrying out an exchange program with Wheaton College (Illinois), which
had a values program with many features similar to
ours. These exchanges proved quite valuable for our

students and for strengthening student support for the program.

Our efforts to gain student organizational support have been generally successful. To our delight, a core of committed students organized their own Values Group to coordinate planning with other student clubs and organizations. The student Values Group quickly gained recognition by the Student Senate as an official student club. Since student planning efforts and activities had to be coordinated with faculty concerns as well, talented and articulate student representatives have participated regularly in the meetings of the Values Group since the fall of 1988.

Although student attendance at Academic Forum events has fluctuated widely, a significant core of approximately sixty students has participated in planning and organizing activities for the forum. Such participation is drawn from various committees of the Student Senate as well as from other student clubs and organizations. In all cases, the Values Group has proceeded on the principle that students are full partners in the planning of events and that their taking responsibility for the success of the program is vital to building student support as a whole.

Admittedly, building student support has been the weakest part of the entire Values Program. The Values Group has not been able to give coordination with student groups the attention it deserves, although the committee has begun to rectify this shortcoming. For a time, we were depressed by our inability to fund the Academic Forum as originally planned. But as one member remarked in reference to another problem, "to a certain extent, we fell into a ditch at midnight, and it turned out to have hot and cold running water and silk sheets." Our experience in this regard leads, therefore, to the very strong recommendation that student help in planning and funding extracurricular events in the program should be requested. Such help can be vital to building strong student support for the Values Program as a whole.

Conclusion

Building institutional support for a program such as this one can be difficult. Problems that arise will certainly be specific to each institution and cannot be predicted universally. There will be setbacks. A values program is ambitious and desirable; but not all that is ambitious and desirable can come to fruition. It is sometimes difficult not to lose patience with administrators or funding agencies who make decisions in view of limited resources. Nevertheless, the broader the support that can be generated among faculty and students, the more "inevitable" and permanent such a program can become. The trick is to take advantage of the fortuitous circumstances that arise and not to become utterly discouraged by the others. It is not easy. It is, however, worth the trouble.

9

Power and Promise: Evaluation of an Evolving Model

"Once there was a little bunny who wanted to run away.
So he said to his mother, 'I am running away.'
'If you run away,' said his mother, 'I will run after you.
For you are my little bunny.'

'If you run after me,' said the little bunny, . . .
'I will be a bird and fly away from you.'
'If you become a bird and fly away from me,'
said his mother, 'I will be a tree that you come home to.'"[1]

The professor looks up at the class. "At which stage of cognitive development would a child be able to comprehend such a passage?" The ensuing discussion explores aspects of cognitive and emotional development, metaphorical reasoning, and the interplay between language and thought. It also brings to light an unanticipated area of student interest. A student asks, "How would a young victim of child abuse feel about this story?" Soon the tone shifts from that of an academic interchange on theories of cognitive development to one of personal engagement. Student questions reveal deep-seated concern for the survival of the cherished child-parent bond in a world of dual-careers and professional day care. Memories of their own childhoods not far behind them, most of the students are nearing a major crossroad with tough choices ahead. The professor appreciates their anxiety, but cannot resolve it. What should, what can, a professor do to enable students to tackle such challenges in productive and morally responsible ways?

The Values Program was born out of such a need. A small group of faculty came together to examine a common feeling of inadequacy in dealing with a basic student need: to develop a way of addressing that dimension of the content in any discipline which poses "what ought to be." At first, the group sought advice by reading literature on values education and by searching for model efforts at other institutions of higher learning. Although it inspired many ideas, the search yielded no satisfactory answers. Thus began Le Moyne's own attempt to articulate appropriate goals and to discover effective means of attaining those goals.

As described in detail in earlier chapters, the Le Moyne approach was based upon an interactive, dual-component model. Faculty would acquire new knowledge and values education skills from an intensive Summer Institute on a given theme, and students would acquire new knowledge and experience with values issues from Academic Forum events on that same theme throughout the year. Thus both faculty and students would meet in the classroom on common ground with shared concerns and complementary skills which would interact in the pursuit of meaningful values education. In order to succeed as a college-wide program, the annual theme had to be stated broadly enough to be relevant across disciplines, and Forum events had to instantiate the theme.

Having begun as a quest, the Values Program became a dynamic effort of discovery rather than the implementation of a proven model. From the beginning, the Values Group recognized the need for objective information to deepen its understanding of values education and for empirical methods to assess the effectiveness of its model. In addition, the group wanted evaluative data that would be more than simply a yardstick for measuring success. The evaluation process was to be analytic in nature so as to yield corrective feedback that would guide the evolution of the model. Our discoveries would then be shared with all professors who feel a sense of inadequacy when faced with students' needs to learn to deal with the values issues inherent in course content, from day care to corporate investments.

Unfortunately, our extensive search of the literature on values education failed to identify an appropriate measurement strategy. Given the innovative character of our enterprise, we were not surprised that suitable instruments could not be found. In fact, our literature search revealed a decided lack of objective information about effective values education and an absence of techniques by which to assess values education programs empirically or to provide corrective feedback for the improvement of those programs. Surely the lack of certainty surrounding how best to accomplish values education is due in part to the lack of methods for empirical evaluation.

Faced with the need to develop a methodology that would serve our purposes as well as provide prototypes for other institutions, we designed techniques that would enhance understanding of effective values education and provide evaluative feedback to improve future Institute and Forum activities. In this chapter, we focus on the evaluation of Institute and Forum activities. We begin with an overview of our assessment approach, and then shift our attention to the lessons learned from that assessment. Finally, we close with a set of conclusions about the power and promise of the Values Program.

Assessment Approach

The primary purpose of the evaluation was to ascertain the extent to which the Values Program brought faculty and students together in effective dialogue about values-laden issues related to their disciplines. We assessed the extent to which the Values Program achieved this goal in terms of the impact of the Summer Institutes and Academic Forums.

As recounted in earlier chapters, the Summer Institutes were intended to enhance faculty's values education skills by exploring pedagogy within the context of a unifying values-laden theme. The themes were economic justice for the 1988 Institute, and peace and war for the 1989 Institute. In order to engender a

sense of ownership, Fellows were free to structure their Institutes in whatever ways they felt would best meet their needs.
For each Institute, three experts in the areas of values education
and thematic content facilitated the Fellows' mastery of the
literature and guided discussion of its pedagogical applications.

The Academic Forums were intended to nurture classroom
discussion of values issues by providing information on some
aspect of the annual theme that would serve as a discussion
vehicle. They were to offer a set of common experiences that Fellows could share with their students during class discussions.
Intended to appeal to the entire academic community as well as
to Institute participants and their students, the Forums were to
validate the Values Program's central assertion that all human
decision making is inevitably based upon a valuative foundation.
With the goals of the Summer Institutes and Academic Forums
in mind, we developed techniques that would:

1. help Fellows participate in the planning of the schedule
   and agenda of their Institute;

2. assess the outcomes or impacts of the Institutes;

3. determine which components of the Institute contributed to its outcomes; and

4. evaluate the impact of the Academic Forums on

   (a) efforts of Fellows to apply their Institute experiences
       to their courses; and

   (b) the academic community in general.

Our assessment approach, therefore, included data collection
at several stages in the development of the Values Program. At
the beginning of each Institute, we gathered information about
the Fellows' goals and expectations. It was clear that while some
outcomes would be evident at the conclusion of each Institute,
others could be assessed only after the Fellows had attempted to
apply their Institute experiences to their courses. In addition,
we wanted to give Fellows the opportunity to reevaluate their Institute experiences in light of these attempts. Consequently, we
obtained data not only at the close of each Institute but also

again after the Fellows had had two semesters during which to implement their new values education strategies.

By the end of the first academic year following their Institute, Fellows were able also to report on the role played by Academic Forum events in their values education efforts. However, full assessment of the college-wide impact of the Academic Forum required information from large samples of faculty and students throughout the college. At the end of the first year of Academic Forum events, we requested this information from all faculty members and from a large sample of students in classes across the curriculum.

Our evaluation of the Values Program, then, consisted of an assessment of the outcomes of the Summer Institutes and Academic Forum. The evaluation of the Summer Institutes was based upon Fellows' responses to three questionnaires: a pretest given at the beginning of the Institute, a posttest given immediately at the end of the Institute, and a follow-up mailed nearly two semesters later. The pretest disclosed Fellows' expectations and goals, and their initial beliefs about how best to allocate their time during the Institute. The posttest revealed the immediate impact of the Institute, and the components of the Institute responsible for that impact. The follow-up revealed the effects of the Institutes on Fellows' courses and teaching practices and on their students' values, values skills, and sensitivity to values concerns. The evaluation of the Academic Forum was based upon information elicited by the follow-up questionnaire on the role that Forum activities played in the classrooms of Institute participants, and upon responses obtained from the general faculty and student body regarding attendance at Forum events and the impact of those events on values analysis skills.

With data from Institute Fellows in particular and faculty and students in general, we were able to examine the usefulness of each component of the Values Program as well as to explore the role of each in relationship to the other. Our approach allowed us to address a number of important questions. For example, were the faculty who participated in the Institutes motivated by the sense of need exhibited by the professor in the scenario at the start of this chapter? Was the Institute experience effective in meeting such a need, and if so, how? What role did the Forum events play? How might the Institute and Forum evolve as integral elements in a Values Program growing in depth and breadth?

The Summer Institutes

The Summer Institutes were designed to incorporate the very features of the educational process which the Fellows would bring back to their classes. Central to this process is an acknowledgement of the student as an active partner in the learning enterprise who retains a sense of ownership in the dynamic interplay between teacher and student. Knowledge is acquired through experience, not simply by way of information transmitted in lectures by the professor. Much thought was given, therefore, to the structure and format of the Institutes as well as to the content to be covered.

Consistent with the aim of having the Fellows retain ownership, Fellows completed *at the start of* the Institute a pretest questionnaire designed to serve as impetus and vehicle for shaping the agenda, structure, and schedule of the Institutes. The pretest also provided baseline data for later comparison with posttest and follow-up responses. The questionnaire contained an open-ended inquiry about the Fellows' goals for the Institutes and a set of structured questions about Fellows' initial expectations and opinions regarding how their time should be allocated. The open-ended inquiry asked Fellows to write a short essay and the structured questions asked them to use rating scales.

Structured items reflected the multidimensional character of both the content and format of the Institutes. We queried Fellows as to how much attention should be given to teaching techniques and applications to their own courses. We then further categorized content into four topics: the theme of economic justice or peace and war, the role of values in education, moral development, and theoretical bases for the development of teaching techniques. We characterized the format of the Institutes as knowledge of the literature, group discussion of the literature, group discussion of personal views, and interaction with experts (i.e., facilitators). Given four types of material which could be treated in each of four ways, there were sixteen possible content/format combinations or features.

Completing the initial questionnaire helped the Fellows articulate their goals and objectives as well as express their expectations and preferences for topics and modes of presentation. In this way, the evaluation process contributed to engaging the Fellows in the Institute experience right from the initial planning and helped ensure that the Institutes were tailored to the expressed needs and interests of the participants.

Expectations

As described by the Fellows in their responses to the open-ended inquiry, participants came searching for effective teaching techniques and for knowledge to help them incorporate values issues into their courses. Both the 1988 and 1989 Fellows were interested in acquiring knowledge about their respective themes of economic justice and peace and war. However, whereas the 1988 Fellows were interested in using the theme primarily as a vehicle for developing values education skills, the 1989 Fellows expressed a relatively greater interest in the theme than in pedagogy. Therefore, while both groups shared a common purpose in wanting to enhance values education, they seemed to differ in their beliefs about how that purpose might best be achieved. The 1988 Fellows emphasized the importance of explicit treatment of pedagogy, and the 1989 Fellows gave greater significance to the role of deeper insights into peace and war issues.

Impact of the Summer Institutes

The difference in approach of the two groups of Fellows is not surprising given how little is known about effective values education and faculty development for that purpose. In an area so dominated by subjective opinion and unsubstantiated theory, it is essential to develop systematic strategies of analysis to strengthen the validity of claims based on self-report alone. While it is interesting to ascertain the extent to which Fellows perceived the Institutes as successful, it is difficult to know how accurate such perceptions can be. Our approach to assessing the impact of the Institutes began with self-report, proceeded with increasingly more structured modes of inquiry, and culminated with statistical analyses to achieve greater objectivity via a system of cross-verification.

Fellows' views of the impact of the Institutes. At the end of each Institute, Fellows were asked to describe what they had gained from the experience. The most frequent responses of Fellows of both Institutes can be categorized into three areas. Most Fellows referred to a greater sense of community with their colleagues which emerged from a deeper appreciation and greater respect for one another. This new sense of solidarity was an unanticipated benefit. In addition, Fellows realized a number of expected gains. Fellows described various benefits to their ability to engage in values education. Some mentioned the acquisition of new pedagogical techniques, some referred to insights into the role of values in their courses, and many expressed enhanced motivation to incorporate values concerns into their courses. Finally, a number of Fellows cited self-improvement in areas such as understanding or appreciation of values issues, especially with respect to the Institutes' themes.

An open-ended format was used to solicit the Fellows' views of which aspects of the Institutes were responsible for its success. A clear pattern of responses emerged common to both Institutes. Fellows cited the opportunity to engage in group discussion as most helpful and the lecture format as least helpful. Most Fellows felt that the practice of dividing into small groups was particularly effective. Fellows credited the facilitators' skills in directing discussion for keeping the Institutes dynamic and stressed the importance of focus, direction, and clarity. It is clear from the open-ended remarks that Fellows perceived the role of the Institutes as one of active involvement in shared inquiry rather than one of information transmission. Consistent with this view, Fellows preferred facilitators to act as guides in the process of exploration, not as sources of expert knowledge.

Impact of the Institutes: A structured inquiry. Our approach emphasizes the question of how success should be defined. Clearly, success should be measured in terms of the degree to which goals are attained. Although the primary ultimate goal of the Institute was that of enhanced values education, a number of objectives can be articulated as means along the way to achieving that end. For example, although the heightened sense of collegiality experienced as a result of the Institutes was an unanticipated gain, it can now be understood as an important dimension of the values education process.

Recognizing the complexity of the Institutes' impact, we defined three criteria or outcomes for the purpose of evaluation. The first criterion was simply the Fellows' perception of the Institutes' success as expressed on a subjective rating scale. This measure reflects the Fellows' overall opinion of the Institutes and can best include benefits which were unanticipated or were unique to individual Fellows. However, such a general judgment lacks the specificity needed to evaluate the impact on the primary goal of enhanced values education. Therefore, the second criterion was a measure of the Fellows' perception of the extent to which the Institutes enhanced their values education abilities, and the third was the reported extent to which the Fellows intended to modify various aspects of their courses as a result of the Institutes.

To measure perceived success, we asked Fellows to rate their Institutes on ten affective scales. Fellows evaluated their Institutes favorably. The Institutes were rated as highly successful, interesting, and pleasant. Positive ratings indicated that Fellows also considered the Institutes to be effective, useful, clear, better than expected, innovative, and rigorous.

Structured questions also assessed the extent to which the Institutes were perceived to have improved the Fellows' ability to engage in values education. All the Fellows believed that the Institutes had improved their ability to help students develop values analysis skills, and most felt that the improvement had been moderate or substantial.

We examined the third outcome, the extent to which the Institutes motivated Fellows to apply the lessons of the Institutes to their teaching, by asking Fellows to rate the degree to which they planned to modify their syllabi, teaching style, reading assignments, and nonreading assignments, and the degree to which they planned to adopt nontraditional teaching techniques. Responses indicated that Fellows intended to implement these modifications in their courses. They anticipated modest change, suggesting that Fellows had realistic expectations for what they could accomplish on the basis of resources gained through the Institutes.

Modest intentions raise a question, however, as to whether the Institutes were effective in making Fellows feel confident in their ability to improve their values education efforts. This concern raises further questions about which aspects of the Institute experience were effective, and whether different outcomes were achieved by different aspects of the experience.

Effective components: Why the Institutes were successful. In order to obtain more specific feedback on particular aspects of the Institute, structured questions elicited subjective ratings of each of the sixteen topic/format combinations. The use of two types of ratings scales allowed Fellows to distinguish between the amount of attention devoted to a feature and the perceived value of that feature. In fact, our analyses showed that Fellows were able to make this distinction and that in many cases the value of the time spent on a feature was independent of the amount of time allocated to it. Furthermore, perceived value was more closely associated with the impact of the Institutes than was the amount of time allocated. It is important, therefore, to be aware of how a topic should be treated in order to ensure quality of time, rather than to design an institute simply in terms of proportion of time allocated to various topics.

Ratings of success, values skills enhancement, and intentions to modify courses reveal the effects of the Institutes, but in themselves do not reveal the components responsible for those outcomes. For example, the finding that both Institutes enhanced participants' values skills does not disclose which components of the Institutes were responsible. Ratings of the value of the time spent on each of the Institute components identify those components Fellows thought valuable, but in themselves do not reveal their impact on outcomes. For example, we found that Fellows in both Institutes thought that the time devoted to teaching techniques was well spent. However, this finding does not in itself imply which outcomes, if any, were produced by effective coverage of teaching techniques.

A component can be thought of as having had a positive impact only if Fellows who thought that the time devoted to that component was well spent experienced better outcomes than did Fellows who were dissatisfied with the attention given to that component. For example, if teaching techniques contributed to enhancement of values skills, then Fellows who thought that the time given to teaching techniques was well spent should experience greater improvement in their values education skills than Fellows who were unhappy with the Institute's coverage of that topic. On the other hand, if Fellows who thought that the Institute's coverage of its thematic content was well done made no more changes in their pedagogy than Fellows who were displeased with the Institute's treatment of its theme, then the pedagogical practices of Fellows could not be said to have been related to the Institute's treatment of content. With this logic, we assessed the impact of each of the Institutes' components by determining whether ratings of the value of time devoted to each component were correlated with ratings of each of the Institutes' outcomes.

A clear pattern emerged from the correlational analyses. Of the topics covered in both Institutes, two—the themes of the Institutes and the role of values in education—had a consistent impact across both groups of Fellows. The nature of the impact of these two topics, however, was very different. Across the two Institutes, effective treatment of thematic content consistently correlated with the Fellows' sense that the Institutes had been successful. However, Fellows who thought that the time devoted to the Institutes' themes was well spent did not report a strengthening of intentions to engage in values education, and experienced an enhancement in values skills only during the 1989 Institute. Effective treatment of the role of values had far broader effects. Across the two Institutes, Fellows who thought that the time devoted to the role of values had been well spent not only felt that their Institute had been a success, but also consistently reported improvement in their values education skills. For the 1988 Fellows, the role of values was correlated also with the intention to apply values education skills to course and teaching modifications. Coverage of theories of moral development and of the theoretical bases of teaching were not related to any impact of either Institute.

Our analysis also shed light on the role played by the outside facilitators. Discussions with facilitators in their role as experts on thematic content correlated with none of the three outcomes, even for the 1989 Fellows, for whom thematic content had been the primary interest. On the other hand, discussions with facilitators about the role of values were related to all outcomes. This finding suggests that outsiders contribute wide-ranging effects by leading discussions of the role of values in education, and is nicely consistent with the Fellows' claim that strengthening belief in the legitimacy of values education was one of the most important aspects of their Institute experiences.

The Institutes' treatment of teaching techniques had very different effects within each Institute. For the 1988 Institute, Fellows who were pleased with the treatment given to teaching techniques felt that the Institute had been a success, experienced an enhancement in values skills, and became committed to engaging in values pedagogy. However, effective treatment of teaching techniques during the 1989 Institute failed to generate any of these outcomes. That discussion of teaching techniques failed to relate to any impact on the 1989 Fellows is made more striking by our finding that these Fellows thought more highly of the treatment given to this topic than did their 1988 counterparts. The reason for this difference is unclear. It might have been that the two groups of participants had different needs, with the 1988 group experiencing a need to learn new pedagogical techniques and the 1989 group a need to learn more about the thematic topic.

On the other hand, even though actual needs might have been similar for the groups, Fellows might have conceptualized different avenues toward the same goal. Consistent with this latter view, despite the lack of relationship between the outcomes and the value of teaching techniques, discussion of the role of values in education was significantly correlated with two of the outcomes for the 1989 Fellows. Perhaps the 1989 group explored pedagogy from the perspective of how values impact on techniques, while the 1988 group approached the question from the perspective of how techniques impact on values. Also consistent with this interpretation, the 1989 Fellows gave a lower estimate of the amount of time allocated to teaching techniques than did the 1988 Fellows, but rated the time spent as more valuable than did the 1988 Fellows.

The 1989 Fellows' lower estimate of the time devoted to teaching techniques was surprising, because in designing the second Institute the director and facilitators planned for greater attention to teaching in light of the importance of that feature in the 1988 Institute. It is possible, however, that the difference between the groups was more perceptual than actual. Having come to the Institutes with different relative priorities, the groups could have perceived the experience in terms of their initial expectations and preferences.

Regardless of the extent to which the two Institutes may have differed in the attention given to teaching techniques, an important issue is the principle of ownership. According to this principle, the Institutes should be customized to the needs of the participants. However, one issue raised by this principle is the validity of the assumption that participants are accurate in their needs assessment and knowledgeable concerning how best to satisfy those needs. For example, one might argue that at least some participants are motivated to attend an Institute by a sense of uncertainty or lack of knowledge concerning values education. Indeed, the Institute experience is expected to yield new insights and perhaps in so doing shift some priorities or bring new possibilities to light. In this sense, then, one might not always expect the "customer" to be right.

The evaluation process yielded some illustrations of such shifts. For example, at the start of the Institutes, interaction with experts on the thematic topic was a very high priority for both groups of Fellows. However, value ratings of these interactions were not reliably related to any of the three outcomes in either Institute. On the other hand, a lower priority component—interaction with experts on the role of values in education—was significantly associated with two of the outcomes for the 1989 Institute and with all three outcomes for the 1988 Institute. One interpretation of these findings suggests that while Fellows may feel a need for expert knowledge in a content area, such knowledge is not sufficient when it comes to actual application for the purpose of values education. The greater need, in fact, was for the experts' facilitation of the values education process itself.

Judgments made at the end of the Institutes could be based only upon anticipations of the real task ahead—applying what had been learned in the Institute to their teaching. Although judgments made after the Institute experience were more informed than the initial perceptions, they were still limited by the uncertainty inherent in being untried and untested. Therefore, we continued the evaluation process by reassessing the impact of Institute features nearly a year following the Institutes. At the time of the follow-up assessment, the Fellows had had two semesters of coursework to which they could apply their newly acquired knowledge and skills.

Impact of the Institutes at Follow-up. The impact of the Institutes on Fellows' teaching was assessed by a follow-up questionnaire. This instrument also gauged the Fellows' sense of the effectiveness of their efforts in enhancing student abilities and afforded them the opportunity to reevaluate their Institute experiences in light of their attempts to apply those experiences to their teaching. In addition, the follow-up elicited information relevant to the evaluation of the Academic Forums. Copies of the follow-up were mailed to Fellows toward the end of the second semester following their respective Institute.

The first part of the questionnaire consisted of open-ended questions which asked Fellows to comment on their experiences as they applied what they had learned during the Summer Institutes to their teaching throughout the fall and spring semesters, and on problems that they might have encountered in using Forum events as a vehicle for discussion of values issues. The second part of the questionnaire was comprised of structured questions assessing the nature and extent of the impact of the Summer Institutes and Forum events on Fellows' courses and teaching practices, on their students, and on their relationships with students and colleagues. Additional structured questions asked Fellows to rate the degree of attention they thought should be given to each Institute component in future summers.

According to the Fellows' responses, the Institutes had had a favorable impact on their role in the classroom, the atmosphere in the classroom, and their relationship with students. Fellows reported somewhat more frequent use of techniques such as group discussion, playing devil's advocate, role-playing, debates and referring to concrete examples or cases. Even more important, perhaps, Fellows reported having somewhat more frequently made references to values issues, integrated economic justice or peace and war issues, and revealed their own values positions. Finally, although small overall, changes in course structure were also reported. Relatively specific aspects such as testing, grading, and course assignments were changed least while relatively more global features such as style and non-traditional methods were changed most.

Although modest, positive effects on students were reported as well. Fellows indicated that the Institutes were useful in improving their ability to help students develop values analysis skills and enhanced values (e.g., strengthened, broadened, made more socially relevant). They also perceived moderate increases in student involvement, interest, and sensitivity to economic justice or peace and war issues and to values concerns in general.

Faculty who increased their use of specific teaching techniques reported an enhancement of students' values and an increase in student responsiveness to values concerns. Faculty who made changes in the structure of their courses reported improvement in student values analysis skills. These findings suggest that both specific teaching techniques and course structure contribute to values education and that their contributions are, at least to some extent, distinct. What a professor does in the classroom can influence the nature of students' values, and can affect motivational and attitudinal variables such as the extent to which they become interested and involved in the course material. Structural components of a course, such as the type of assignments, tests, etc., engage students in tasks which can enable them to develop and exercise values analysis skills.

Although the changes that Fellows' introduced were not extensive and the impact of those changes were modest, Fellows' indicated that they intend to continue to change aspects of their teaching. The extent of further change Fellows planned to implement was moderate, yet these intentions are noteworthy, given that they were present after nearly a year of attempts at such change. In fact, their intentions at follow up were at least as strong as they had been at the end of the Institute or, in the case of reading assignments, stronger. It appears that the Institutes engendered among Fellows a long-term commitment to enhancing values education, and that Fellows did not consider their efforts to improve their values education pedagogy to be complete.

Having tried to apply what they had learned to their courses, the Fellows rated nearly all aspects of the experience somewhat useful, but they perceived the degree of impact of many components as being quite modest. The material which they thought most helpful was that on teaching techniques, applications to courses, and the role of values in education. Despite the fact that these Fellows at the close of the Institutes had been satisfied with the attention that had been given to pedagogy and thematic content, they came to believe that the Institutes' treatment of pedagogy had not been sufficient and that material on thematic content had not been as useful as they had anticipated. Many recommended that future Institutes should devote more attention to actual teaching techniques and to concrete examples of classroom applications, and some wrote of the difficulties they encountered in courses to which the Institute themes were not directly related.

Summary of the Summer Institutes

Overall, the pattern of results exhibits greater similarity than dissimilarity between the two Institutes. Despite some initial differences between the groups of Fellows, both Institutes enhanced the practice of values education and did so by giving Fellows TLC—teaching techniques, legitimacy, and content. Explicit consideration of teaching techniques was related to a number of positive effects during and following the 1988 Institute, and was felt by both 1988 and 1989 Fellows at follow-up to be crucial to successful attempts at applying values education skills to coursework.

The second influential factor contributing to the impact of the Institutes was the strengthening of a sense of legitimacy with respect to values education. The importance of this element was revealed on several levels. On a personal level, Fellows gained the confidence to engage in values education as they became empowered with enhanced abilities, sharper insights, and new pedagogical techniques. On a more fundamental level, one of principle, Fellows acquired a strengthened conviction that values education is appropriate—especially within the individual's own discipline. This conviction developed from the experience of public affirmation which grew out of discussions of personal views with colleagues and interaction with experts from outside the institution. The presence of facilitators who were respected authority figures was critical as a new, independent source of legitimacy. When it came time to implement change, however, this principle-based conviction might have faltered if it had been dependent solely upon an external authority. A renewed sense of community which developed among the Fellows provided the courage and support needed to meet the challenge of implementing change.

The third effective component of the Institutes, the thematic content, functioned primarily as a vehicle by which discussion of teaching techniques and the legitimacy of values education could be focused and advanced by the use of a common subject matter. Although the use of a single theme simplified the logistics of managing an Institute, it made application to courses difficult for those faculty who teach in disciplines with content highly dissimilar to the Institute theme. Thus, although most Fellows valued the exploration of the thematic topic, some discovered that their Institute skills did not transfer easily to the content of their courses.

Although more may have to be done to help participants effectively cross content boundaries, the Institutes provided insights and skills that Fellows hoped to bring to a receptive student audience interested in and informed by events they had attended outside the classroom. The creation, coordination, and presentation of these events were the responsibility of the Values Program's second component, the Academic Forum.

The Academic Forum

The Academic Forums were established to extend the values education process college-wide by making opportunities to explore the issues integral to the unifying theme available to all community members. By using a mix of formats that included plays, lectures, films, and panel discussions, Forum events were designed to motivate students to address values issues in different contexts and from a variety of perspectives. The unifying theme allowed for coordination between the Institutes and Fellows' classes as well as across disciplines. Equally important, each event was to enhance values analysis skills by demonstrating, if only indirectly, the values structures that underlie human affairs.

In light of the important role played by the Forum in the Values Program, information was gathered from the faculty and student body at large to assess the effectiveness of the Forum in supporting the impact of the Institute and in extending values education throughout the college. Since the second Academic Forum is still in progress at the time of this writing, the observations made here apply to the first Forum on the theme of economic justice.

We measured the success of the Forum by three criteria: the number of students and faculty who participated in its events, the extent to which this participation enhanced values skills, and the ability of Fellows to incorporate students' Forum experiences into their classes. To assess the first two outcomes at the end of the academic year, we mailed copies of a survey to all faculty and distributed copies in classes to over five hundred students. This survey asked respondents to check which of a series of forty campus events they had attended during the preceding two semesters. Respondents also rated the impact of each event attended on their values analysis skills. The events, twenty Forum sponsored and twenty nonForum, were listed in chronological order without any labelling or clustering to identify them as Forum or nonForum events. The third outcome, the impact of the Forum on the classes of Fellows, was explored in the follow-up questionnaire used in the evaluation of the Summer Institutes.

Over one-half of the 466 students we sampled and over half of the seventy-six faculty members who returned our questionnaire reported attending at least one Forum event. Attendance at Forum events was as good as at non-Forum events during the same academic year, which included popular events such as the senior show. These figures suggest that the Forum had significant appeal for the general academic community.

Given the differences in interests between faculty and students, among faculty, and among students, it is not surprising that the pattern of attendance figures across events was not identical for all audiences. Events which had greater appeal among faculty were not equally attractive among students. Student attendance at extracurricular events in general varied with the student's major discipline. Attendance at Forum events surveyed was highest for students majoring in the humanities, and next highest for majors in the social sciences, then natural science, and business. However, humanities majors were also most likely and business majors least likely to attend events not sponsored by the Academic Forum. This finding suggests that humanities and business majors differ in their general tendency to participate in extracurricular activities and implies that the planning of future Forum activities may have to include consideration of how to appeal to students who are not predisposed to taking advantage of out-of-class opportunities.

This same pattern of differences in attendance by discipline was also evident among the faculty for campus events not associated with the Forum. However, Forum events were best attended by faculty in the social sciences, followed by those in the humanities, business, and the natural sciences. Perhaps this difference in the appeal of the Forum was due to differences in the perceived relevance of its theme, economic justice, to the content of courses that social and natural scientists teach. Faculty presence at extracurricular activities was related also to participation in the Summer Institute. Fellows attended more events than did other faculty and this difference was especially true for the events of the Academic Forum.

While attendance is critical for exposure to occur, it is an incomplete index of effectiveness. Effectiveness of an event is mainly determined by the quality of the values education which occurs during the event, while attendance depends on such factors as time of the semester, competing events, or responsibilities (e.g., midterms), and type and extent of the marketing of the event. To assess the usefulness of the Forum in terms of values education more completely, we examined faculty and student ratings of the extent to which each event attended improved their values analysis skills.

Whereas the patterns of attendance at events were not highly similar for faculty and students, the ratings of events by faculty and students were more closely related. For both faculty and students, Forum events on the average were rated as having improved values analysis skills to a greater extent than did non-Forum events. This distinction of the value of Forum and non-Forum events did not vary by major of the student or by discipline of the faculty member. According to these ratings, therefore, Forum events succeeded in improving values analysis skills to a greater degree for both faculty and students than did ordinary campus events.

Interaction:
Academic Forum and Summer Institute

Given the agreement between faculty and students that the Forum events served as vehicles for the development of values analysis skills, it is clear that the Forum was successful in addressing one of the objectives of the Values Program. Opportunities for values education were made available to the entire college community. An important question remains, however. With its unifying theme, did the Forum provide the link between student and professor, especially between student and Institute Fellow?

Pertinent information came from responses to open-ended questions on the follow-up questionnaire. Many Fellows reported either very little or no effect of the Forum on their efforts to incorporate values issues into their teaching. In most cases, they attributed this lack of impact to difficulty incorporating material and issues from the Forum events into their courses, and offered two major reasons for this difficulty. On a simple level, Fellows remarked that they could not make contact on common ground, because not all their students had attended the events. On a more complex level, Fellows themselves were not always capable of integrating the Forum content into courses in unrelated areas. On the positive side, Fellows praised the Forum for motivating them by reinvigorating their own interest in and sensitivity to values concerns.

Summary of the Academic Forum

The Academic Forum consisted of a series of activities which provided values education experiences to both faculty and students. Of further importance, the unifying theme was of special value to those Fellows who taught courses in which content related to the Forum theme was integral. Two primary obstacles interfered with attaining the intended goals of interaction between Institute and Forum and of establishing common ground between professors and students.

The first obstacle, poor attendance at campus events, can be addressed at several levels. For example, attention could be given to improved marketing strategies to increase awareness and interest throughout the college. Greater involvement of faculty and students in the planning of the events could be encouraged to expand the sense of ownership and to facilitate the development of activities which address interests and needs of the college community. On a more individualized level, faculty could consider incentives to ensure attendance at the particular events they plan to incorporate into their courses. This last strategy is of special interest in light of the finding that the attractiveness of an event differed between faculty and students and among students majoring in different fields. Generalized marketing strategies disseminated college-wide are not likely to succeed with different groups, and differential attendance interferes with the realization of the Forum's intended role as link between student and professor.

The second obstacle, difficulty incorporating issues across content boundaries, is more fundamental and troublesome. Increased attendance will not solve this problem. In fact, this obstacle is reminiscent of the difficulty encountered by Fellows trying to implement what they had learned in the Institute into courses with content unrelated to the Institute theme. Although values education skills may be able to transfer from one content area to another, it is not clear how easy or how difficult such transfer is or even to what extent such transfer actually occurred for the Fellows. Consideration must be given to the problem of crossing content boundaries if the college-wide impact of the Forum as a link between professor and student is to be strengthened.

Conclusions

Having followed dedicated professors and students through a year of effort, we have learned much about the power of the Values Program to enhance the practice of values education. We discovered that the yearning expressed by the scenario professor for the confidence and ability to help students deal with weighty values issues is typical of the motivation that brings faculty to the Institutes and keeps their efforts alive throughout a challenging year of implementation. We learned that the Summer Institutes can satisfy this yearning and produce a community of faculty who feel empowered to address values issues without sacrificing academic integrity. The techniques that participants bring to the classroom can influence the nature of students' values, and can encourage students to become more actively involved in the learning process. While what professors do in the classroom can enhance student motivation, what students do can enhance their ability to engage in fruitful values analysis.

The Summer Institutes work best when endowed with TLC—teaching techniques, legitimacy, and content—with the primary emphases on teaching and legitimacy. Time devoted to mastery of thematic material enhances the participants' sense of the Institute's effectiveness immediately at its close, but is not related to their values education practices or their impact on students later on. Content, therefore, serves as a vehicle for discussion, but can impede the application of newly acquired skills if boundaries must be crossed without assistance.

Empowerment is heightened by a sense of control or ownership. However, we have learned that despite the importance of ownership, the customer is not always right. When expressing their needs, faculty can overestimate the significance of thematic content while underestimating their need to discuss teaching techniques and to have peers and respected outsiders affirm the appropriateness of values as a subject of discourse within their courses.

Perhaps most important, the Values Program has demonstrated the feasibility of bringing together individuals of very different areas of expertise in dialogue on issues of common concern. While challenging problems exist in bridging differences in interest and content, the Academic Forum can enhance values analysis skills in faculty and students and illustrates a promising vehicle for bringing faculty and students together in meaningful discussion.

Together, the Institute and Forum can help create an enriched learning environment in which values education occurs within a dynamic interplay between student and professor. With time, these two components should evolve to an even more functionally integrated enterprise. Innovative strategies can be developed to link areas of the curriculum unrelated to the thematic content to values inquiry by creating clusters of active explorers, each focused on a theme of personal significance. Over time, a more fully evolved Values Program will not only expose all members of the college community to new themes and new ways of studying a particular theme, but it will also encourage all to maintain a long-standing interest in and dedication to a theme as they are reinvigorated by fresh insights derived from their exposure to new concepts.

We have learned, then, that much has been achieved and so much more lies ahead. With the creation of the Values Program, Le Moyne has successfully taken the first step toward the realization of its ambitious dreams.

And so it came to be that when it was time again to teach about metaphorical reasoning in young children, the professor anticipated with greater confidence the haunting questions the students would raise. The professor begins reading,

"This is a Remarkable Rabbit. He thinks he will run away. . .

And this is the Remarkable Rabbit running and jumping away.

But he falls into a deep dark hole.
In the hole are
  a frog
   a snake
    a worm
     and a porcupine . . .

He jumps up and pops out of that hole so fast
you can hardly see little Remarkable Rabbit running
down the road.
And he runs and he runs and he runs
  to his Mother.

'I'll never fall into a big black hole again,'
he says.
'Don't be silly,' says his Mother. 'You'll fall
into plenty of holes. Just remember that you can
always get yourself out of them. You are a
Remarkable Rabbit. Never forget that.' "[2]

Endnotes

1. Margaret Wise Brown, *The Runaway Bunny*, (New York: Harper & Row Publishers, 1977), pp. 1-2, 14-15.

2. Margaret Wise Brown, "A Remarkable Rabbit," in *Once Upon A Time in a Pigpen,* (Reading, MA: Addison-Wesley, 1980), pp. 19, 21-22, 32.

10

The Essential
"Inc-Factor"

What, in a nutshell, is Le Moyne's Values Program approach?

Re-emphasizing its commitment to the importance of values in the educational process, Le Moyne College has established a multiyear program which assists faculty, students, and administrators to develop an understanding of social, economic, and political issues in ways that incorporate a serious consideration of values.

So states an informative brochure introducing the very effective Values Program at Le Moyne College. I have had the honor of working with some of Le Moyne's faculty, administrative, and student leaders on various occasions, including the exchange program with Wheaton College (Illinois) mentioned in chapter 8. Mine is an "outsider's" perspective on this engaging program.

The sentence quoted above briefly and accurately describes important aspects of the program, especially its most potent quality: what can truly be called the *incarnation* of values "in the educational process." This includes the *incorporation* of responsible values reflection within social, economic, and political understanding so clearly emphasized in the brief statement. The concrete embodiment (and incorporation) of values conveys the essential "incarnation-factor"—or "inc-factor"—that especially explains the distinctive effectiveness, competence, and substance of Le Moyne's program. I will first identify the elements of this inc-factor and show its importance to the program. In the second section I explain two ways in which this inc-factor can become even more potent at Le Moyne and at other colleges.

Elements

There are at least four crucial elements of the incarnation factor evident in this informative book and in Le Moyne's Values Program. The first is *involvement*. While a portion of the leadership of the Program comes from the ethics experts in philosophy and religion, the weight of leadership is broadly shared, including members of virtually every department and organization of the college. Even students, administrators, and student development staff are included with faculty in both participatory leadership and enthusiastic involvement. As you have read in chapter 8, some of the breadth of this involvement was made necessary initially because of a lack of funds, but this prenatal "poverty" procreated a distinguishing feature of Le Moyne's fruitful Values Program.

Although my own qualifications as an "ethicist" come from extensive training in philosophy and theology, I have come to see these two disciplines as potentially distorting lenses. It is probably quite obvious to most nonphilosophers and most nontheologians that there are "precious few" actual philosophical or theological ethical issues. Instead, our values issues are concrete human concerns. They must involve everyone. And responsible understanding of the complexities and nuances of ethical issues always involves multiple disciplines.

Philosophical and theological ethics are both empty and misguided without significant input from the other academic disciplines. If you think about it, many disciplines give not only facts for informed ethical decision making, but also perspective, vision for new behavioral directions, standards of comparison, and the like. Some academic disciplines even furnish helpful values criteria—for example, a healthy habitat in biology, fair exchange in economics, wholeness of persons and relationships in psychology and sociology, and the like. Ethical issues are not well understood apart from a broad perspective and honest multidisciplinary insight.

The considerable involvement of faculty, students, and administrators has saved the Le Moyne Values Program from the dangerous dominance of detached theoretical or specialized ethics. Instead, values are encountered within down-to-earth problems and comprehended in multidisciplinary perspectives. This concrete engagement has kept the program both "real" and memorable for students and faculty.

The second element of Le Moyne's "incarnation factor" is *thoughtful convergence*. Too often in a pluralistic environment, the kind of setting in which private colleges like Le Moyne find themselves, faculty and student development staff are hesitant to teach ethics. Of course, if faculty think about such an effort in terms of the indoctrination model of values education, they are wisely reluctant to become involved. They do not want to be presumptuous or to seem pushy, and they do not want others to be dogmatic.

The sphere of ethical values, like any important area of our lives, involves some significant points of disagreement. For example, present quarrels over abortion and capital punishment are real and not easily resolved. However, these cases are not typical of values issues. They are exceptions to the "general rule" of our lives, for convergent values are the dominant pattern in our experience.

For the most part, we all work daily with a prodigious values convergence. We can immediately recognize many diverse forms of theft, murder, and deceit. When such unacceptable behavior appears in literature, drama, movies, television, and even real life news and experience, there is rarely even a hint of debate concerning its moral worth. The moral categories of such acts are rarely matters of controversy.

More important, values like courage, care, efficiency, and justice are also repeatedly recognized with ease in the plethora of behavior in daily life and in depictions in literature, art, and various dramatic forms. With only rare exceptions, the applications of these values terms are noncontroversial. Ethical theories in philosophy and theology far too frequently do us the tragic disservice of presuming profound disagreement between values perspectives. By contrast, the actual prevailing convergence of values provides a positive context for debate, and the pluralism of personal and professional perspectives helps make our values debate fruitful.

Without a doubt, this prevailing convergence of our habitual value judgments is no guarantee of their infallibility. Nor does it deny existent differences in approaches or specific cases. However, the values convergence provides the indispensable insurance for our common values language—the language that enables our dialogue and debate about ethical issues to be intelligent, purposeful, and beneficial. Equipped with this prevalent bona fide convergence of our value judgments, our actual disagreements can generally be pointed and specific. Ever since as three-year-olds we first fussed with our parents and siblings about proper uses of toys and fair servings of milk or chocolate cake, shared values have been an elemental part of our world. Since we talk and work together, we must have similar value judgments.

It is, perhaps, their "rediscovery" of this common values language—and this prevailing thoughtful convergence of values in concrete situations and cases—that empowers the faculty, students, and administrators at Le Moyne College to engage each other in such refreshingly cogent, fruitful values discovery and dialogue. And this convergence is not theory-dependent, but emanates from a common concrete task—that of bringing a college together.

Character development provides the third element of Le Moyne's "incarnation factor" in effective values education. Lectures, discussions, and debates can contribute to the development of personal values character, and Le Moyne's program includes many of these. However, its multidisciplinary approach also includes coordinated student theater and arts programs, retreat activities, and liturgical celebrations—all creatively integrated with the annual values theme. A full range of human experience is touched and expressed.

In its very form, the Values Program is not a detached addition but incarnated into the broad curriculum, for most of these particular intellectual, artistic, social, and religious events would have occurred anyway. There is virtually no additional work involved. But there is the sense of esprit that has nurtured cooperation and shared vision on Le Moyne's campus. And this cooperative spirit itself is exemplary of the values character Le Moyne seeks to model for its students.

Nevertheless, two elements of Le Moyne's incarnate character development are conscious additions to the broader curriculum. On the one hand, students organize campus simulation activities to help expand their own awareness of values needs. For example, you have read that during the year on economic justice they staged a creative three-day campus-wide simulation of apartheid, complete with identity card distribution, restricted areas, police raids, protests, boycotts, identity card burning, and the like. To the narrowly theoretical mind, such simulations may seem so safe, short, and cute as to be worthless imitations of the real values challenge they mimic. Nevertheless, such well-directed simulations potently stretch imaginations, give a genuine feel for the "incarnate" issues, and help people symbolically—even "liturgically"—identify with critical challenges and sufferings.

On the other hand, the element of character development is vital for the Values Group and the Values Program itself. Early in the committee's work a commitment was made to make research and evaluation an integral element of the Program's activities. This internal evaluation has been professional, thorough, and even brutally honest, as it is supervised by faculty members with expertise in measurement and statistical analysis. It is their way of incarnating their best professional tools in an especially worthy task. Such thorough, honest self-evaluation is also an integral part of any developed individual or group moral character.[1]

The fourth and final incarnational element that I wish to point out in the Values Program is *free play*. There is nothing stuffy or rigid about its approach: the Values *Program* is *not* *"programmed."* Le Moyne has discovered enough thoughtful convergence to get people talking about values, and enough free play to keep the conversation lively. It is a shared, coordinated, integrated program because of common purposes—quality liberal arts in the Jesuit tradition. Given this coordinated vision, the excitement and vitality of the program is enhanced by the free play of pluralism within the college and the program itself. Because the commitment to values is so incarnated into the present life processes for the college, it is expressed freely. When we know what we are doing together, our trust increases—our trust in each other and in the free play of our professional work. And Le Moyne College knows what it is doing.

"Environmental" Resources

Le Moyne's incarnation factor is essential to its Values Program. The benefits of this inc-factor can be increased even more in at least two ways that involve strengthening the ties of the college with its community. In short, Le Moyne can fruitfully rediscover its own local incarnation.

First, the Le Moyne program would be enhanced through additional contact with local "values practitioners." My own experience in organizing collegiate ethics activities has been in the Chicago and New York City areas. However, I am confident that the Syracuse community has a wealth of familiar untapped resources that the Le Moyne Values Program can cultivate.

In almost any community in which a college or university finds itself there are honest, thoughtful, articulate "practitioners" of values who are excellent resources for effective values programs. Corporate executives, public officials (judges, legislators, school board members, city planners), and religious leaders often must spend so much time developing and fulfilling the basic directions of their offices that they explicitly think and act upon values on a day-to-day basis. They are, perhaps, "ethicists with power."

Not just any executive, public official, or religious leader will do, however. It takes time to develop networks of people who understand the purposes of values programs in a liberal arts setting. Different members of a college or university values group can help cultivate relationships within particular groups of practitioners. Some of these contacts are probably already established through existing community and professional activities of values group members. Values practitioners can be found who can dialogue honestly and informatively with intellectuals and students without insulting audiences with trite or self-serving pronouncements.

The effectiveness of activities in a values program depends on the selection of the right people and the development of effective settings. One type of effective setting is what I have called a "trialogue workshop" involving practitioners, scholars, and students. For example, a scholar can give a lecture on a particular theme, with a panel of two or three practitioners serving as respondents. Alternatively, a practitioner could lecture, with the respondent panel drawn primarily from faculty or guest scholars. Quality cooperation is enhanced when copies of the lecture are available for respondents at least two weeks in advance. Surprisingly, I have found that the right practitioners will generally take more thoughtful effort preparing for such a discussion than scholars.

Practitioners help scholarly discussions focus on concrete issues and real resolutions. *Scholars*—faculty and guest scholars—help practical discussions examine significant issues in a broad context of understanding. *Students* can keep discussions honest and stimulating. All three parts of the "trialogue" are valuable. If the expectations of the trialogue forum are understood ahead of time, people can disagree in informative and stimulating ways. I have organized dozens of such trialogue discussions, and they have generally been immensely fruitful for all the participants.

Values program leaders will find a reservoir of good feeling and interest among the "movers and shakers" who serve as values practitioners in almost any community. And, because these practitioners enjoy such occasional interaction with young bright minds, many will gladly participate with little or no remuneration.

A second way in which the Le Moyne program could be enhanced is through occasional topical courses in "live" case studies; the topic could be coordinated with the particular year's values theme. Unfortunately, the case studies some of us use in our regular class teaching are already partly digested: the problems and dilemmas are predefined, and relevant facts are already collected, isolated, and carefully stated. Such case studies are immensely useful for teaching complex decision-making skills[2], but they remain several levels of abstraction away from our actual ethical dilemmas.

Upper-level students could well engage their minds and hearts in a course equipping them with various personal and intellectual resources and launching them in teams to work on a particular live ethical dilemma. They could pick a dilemma that is presently challenging various people in the region near the college. The college might find itself already involved in some of these dilemmas. Students could research the particular issues, interview various players in the complex setting, observe behavior, attempt to define the problems and options, expose the values at stake, and thoughtfully explore possible resolutions.

For example, when family issues provide a given year's theme, two or three students in such a class could team together on each of several specific problems—latch-key children, poverty, child abuse, and the like. They could interview children and adults affected by these problems, investigate the social and structural conditions that influence or aggravate these conditions, dialogue with representatives from various helping agencies actually engaged with these concerns, confer with political and religious leaders, and evaluate recommended changes and policies. Local live cases can be found for almost any kind of ethical dilemma.

Let me give some specific examples from my own experiences organizing and helping to teach such a class at Wheaton College. Under the theme of ecology, one team of students prepared a case based on the problems and resources for waste disposal in a particular neighborhood of Chicago. After some preliminary class meetings about ethical standards, pollution problems, and interview techniques, this team interviewed concerned neighbors of a waste processing facility, a Chicago alderman, a city planner, scientists, and engineers. They also visited the community to observe the problems several times before producing an interesting and responsible report. In the same class other students wrote their investigative case studies on the history and problems of flood control policy for a particular suburb, the aesthetic and ecological impacts of a particular housing development under construction, and so forth.

For another class, under the theme of economic development, a team of students investigated the complex challenges and the history of failures in one of the three poorest neighborhoods of Chicago. They interviewed several residents, ministers, physicians, a psychologist, and some business people in the neighborhood, as well as the local alderman and state representative. All these important people were eager to help by sharing their knowledge and special perspectives. The psychologist even closed down his entire clinic for ninety minutes to allow the students to interview himself and all his assistants in one intense group. As in the "trialogue workshops" described above, local "values practitioners" are usually eager to help with such a case studies class. Contact with these experts can strengthen further the all-important "incarnation factor" for effective values programs.

Final Perspective

Le Moyne is serious about values education—so serious that it has actively engaged a huge portion of its faculty, students, administration, and student development staff; so serious that every part of the college is quite conscious of the annual value-laden theme; and so serious that large teams work hard—including three weeks every summer—to study and plan for effective efforts and activities for the coming year.

This Values Program lives and breathes. It is incarnate within Le Moyne's purposes, classes, student activities, arts productions, faculty development, and within its own self-consciousness and self-assessment. But how else could such an effective values program work?

Endnotes

1. For further discussion of the necessity of feedback loops for responsible ethical thought, see Paul de Vries, "Godel, Gadamer, and Moral Business Leadership: Strange Loops, Hermeneutical Circles, and Invisible Hands," *Business and Professional Ethics Journal,* Vol. 5, No. #3 & #4.

2. For a detailed analysis of the benefits of case studies, see Paul de Vries, "The Discovery of Excellence: The Assets of Exemplars in Business Ethics," *Journal of Business Ethics,* June, 1986.

Conclusion

11

From Vision to Action

The story of the Le Moyne Values Program is one of "ambitious dreams," of daring imaginings and forays into the unknown. The explorers were not men and women of mythic proportions but a grass-roots group of six faculty and one administrator in a Jesuit college in the eastern part of the United States. Although we did not realize it then, we were about to begin a process which has lasted five years so far—and which has begun to revitalize the ethos and culture of the entire institution. Through this book we have invited you to share our journey: to understand why we began the voyage, what preparations were necessary, how others came to join us, and what we discovered on the way.

The Values Group originated as, and still remains, a grassroots group. The project evolved from the bottom up through the efforts of an ad hoc working group, with no official status in the college, whose members came together through their own initiative. We were not a committee mandated to return a report or a proposal; nor were we an arm of the Faculty Senate, the Curriculum Committee or an academic department. We were not connected to any part of the administration, trustees, or the founding religious order (the Jesuits). Rather, we were a backyard movement, a group of faculty tinkering in the garage on Saturdays and after hours, a people's popular front.

In retrospect, this grass-roots beginning provided us with freedom to develop at our own pace, to search out various alternatives when constructing programs, targeting funding sources, etc. It also freed us from much of the immediate politics of the college. Because we were not an arm of the president's or the dean's office, we had to create our own institutional base. Our base did not derive from the power of office but from our ability to convince others of the worth of our idea. The fact that we worked without reward, remuneration, or prestige contributed to our credibility in the college.

As a grass-roots group, we had to work hard to convince administrators that ours was a project worth supporting. With no line in the official school budget and no advocate at the weekly meetings for administrative heads, we certainly were not traditional power brokers. Having to raise funds and convince various administrative and faculty groups to help our efforts during the first four years caused the Values Group to think creatively about how best to present our case. We did not realize it then, but we were building the first tentative connections among various constituencies in the college.

Because an educational institution's ethos shapes the moral consciousness of its participants, it is important to examine how that institution's members actually experience their work and the educational process.[1] For many of our faculty and students, the experience had been one of incoherence, fragmentation, and disintegration. The question we faced was how to move the individual and the institution in the direction of coherence, community, and integration. This program has been described as a new means of educating, one with the power to inject new energy into scholarship, teaching, and research, and to bring about significant and strategic institutional change. Since the model is in process and evolving, any claims are still tentative. In this conclusion I would first like to focus on a question often raised by educators and parents learning about our program: how does one respect academic freedom while arguing for commitment to a specific worldview and set of values? Next, I will comment on what we have accomplished—how we have moved from vision to action. Four areas deserving special consideration are: the program as model, college-wide morale building, hiring and promotion practices, and the interaction between academics and student life. Following this, I shall address the challenges that lie ahead for the Values Program.

From its beginning the Values Program at Le Moyne was exploratory in nature. Our original Values Group had very few answers and many questions. So we began at a fundamental level, asking ourselves what we thought appropriate objectives in values education might be. Only after agreeing on an answer to that question could we work to discover effective means of attaining those objectives. We knew from the start that we faced a great challenge. How, after all, does one motivate students to explore issues and learn skills that lie beyond their careers and personal needs?

The most elusive and troubling area we confronted in our discussions involved deciding which values and values issues we should focus on. The more we interacted as a group, listened to each other, and came to trust one another's motives, intuitions, and intentions, the more we recognized the necessity for respecting each other's freedom and individuality. Our experience in interacting as a group while grappling with complex and very personal attitudes towards values confirmed our stand against educational practices which might indoctrinate students into accepting a particular set of theories or beliefs.

This brings me to the question which resonates throughout the program and is one of its greatest sources of energy and tension: how does one respect the personal, professional, and institutional freedom and integrity of the student and professional educator—staff, faculty, or administrator—while arguing that all involved in education must commit to a specific worldview and set of values? For more than two years this issue was at the center of our group debates. We resolved it to our satisfaction by arriving at three principles: (1) people do need to commit themselves to a framework of values; (2) the framework must be consistent and defensible to themselves and consonant with the best of the human community's traditions; and (3) knowledge leads to choice and responsible social action.

The Values Program provides a model for higher education which insists upon the "value of values" as a norm for faculty, administrators, and staff in contemporary higher education. Our program contains the seeds for a "new species" of college or university, where teaching, scholarship, and research are understood as deeply rooted in values concerns and where the search for truth leads one to choices which are acted upon. We insist on the "value of values," the absolute centrality and necessity of values to all dimensions of human life, including the academic enterprise. Our main premise is that values be given a central place in inquiry and action. After all, values concerns permeate all aspects of the human condition.

Some will say that we have merely rediscovered and revitalized the traditional understanding of the liberal arts. Others will argue that the challenges faced by higher education and scholarship are so new that old answers and old approaches no longer satisfy. This book is not written to argue one way or another. We only assert that a values program can reorient faculty, administrators, and students in ways more appropriate to serving the contemporary world.

The instrument which provided this spark of creativity is a deceptively simple prototype model with two interactive components—the Summer Institute and the Academic Forum—which constitute a critical accomplishment of the Values Program. It will be recalled that the primary purpose of these components is to bring faculty and students together in effective dialogue about values-laden issues relevant to their disciplines and lives. The results of the evaluation of the 1988 and 1989 Institutes indicate that both have been successful. For example, most participants felt that the program enhanced values education in their classrooms and enabled them to help students deal with weighty values issues. The Summer Institutes also produced a community of faculty who felt empowered to enhance students' values skills by modifying teaching techniques and changing course structures. One of the mysteries of education has always been how to motivate students to act in accordance with the best of what they see and understand. We do not pretend to have a magic solution, but as I will suggest at the close, this project as it has evolved is itself a model of moral courage for our students.

A second area where the Values Program has attained positive results is in the building and maintaining of morale, resulting in large part from members of the college community believing that the program is unique and worth one's loyalty. In fact, the Values Program's impact on faculty morale may be its most significant, and unforeseen, accomplishment. Such outcomes as increased quality of colleagueship; richer, more frequent activity among faculty in different disciplines; greater enthusiasm deriving from grant awards; and an evolving sense that the college is at the forefront of a much wider educational process, nationally and internationally, have all helped to create better morale. Through the Summer Institute and the Academic Forum, an improved morale has begun to spread throughout the institution. The personal perspectives by Bob Kelly and Bill Miller (chapters 5 and 6), two faculty who knew little of the project until they became participants in the first Summer Institute on economic justice (1988), attest to the impact this program has had on individuals and groups of faculty. But the effect on morale is not confined to faculty: it reaches all constituencies of the college, including staff, students, and administrators. Various offices such as counseling and minority student affairs, residence life, and student life have become involved. Gradually, a sense has been building up within the institution that we have something different to offer that distinguishes us from other colleges.

Closely related to the issue of morale in the college community is the third area—that of hiring and promotion practices. Any institution must pay special attention to the criteria that actually function in those practices because it is through hiring and promotion that the college—or any organization—constantly readjusts its nature. Moreover, these practices determine to a great extent the future direction of the college or university, functioning like switches in a railroad yard. We need to affirm that no professions or situations are devoid of values. Therefore, our institutional commitment to values must function as a major norm and criterion for hiring and promotion. All those applying for positions in the college must not only be open to the "need for values" but also willing, motivated, and sufficiently courageous to conduct themselves in their professional and career activities in a way reflective of values consciousness.

The impact of the Values Program on the hiring and promotion process has been slow and almost imperceptible, but definite. Published job descriptions now reflect this impact with phrases like "mission of the college," "concern for values," "student-centered teaching," and "the need for diversity." The program also encourages certain kinds of applicants. Administrative searches now are concerned with how the actions of a potential dean or member of the student life staff might mesh with the ethos of the college. We hope that highly sought after faculty candidates will be attracted by the college's distinctive and visible commitment to values in education. Ultimately, a values program can make a college more attractive to applicants for faculty and staff positions precisely because of this dimension.

Finally, a very subtle but effective change resulting from the Values Program has been the increased interaction between the faculty and student life personnel. When we began the project, we as faculty felt powerless to significantly affect student life outside the classroom, even though our college is small (two thousand students) and even though we served on various boards dealing with commuters and resident students. A positive change occurred when we invited the associate dean for minority affairs and the director of counseling into our group. We learned from them how to begin to work effectively with student life staff to achieve shared goals. One example of this cooperative activity occurred at the most recent annual meeting of the National Association for Student Personnel Administrators (NASPA). Their theme this year was "Creating an Ethical Climate on Campus." One session consisted of a panel from Le Moyne: a faculty member, a student resident advisor, and the director of student life.

The Institutes and the Academic Forum demand short- and long-range planning, very hard work, and careful attention to minute detail if they are to be successful. All through this book are examples of hard work by people willing to sacrifice time and energy to effect necessary change. The difficult process of finding the right facilitators for the Summer Institute, for example, usually takes about a year to complete. Similarly, the process of involving students in the activities—especially commuter and other nontraditional students—requires much planning, creativity, and perseverance.

Looking to the future, two primary, continuous tasks remain for the Values Program. The first involves improving the Values Program at Le Moyne; the second relates to developing, marketing, and disseminating the program to other institutions. These tasks require quite different approaches.

The interacting dual components of the Values Program were created, developed, and implemented specifically for Le Moyne. To assess program implementation and impact at Le Moyne, we developed a comprehensive research and evaluation component under the leadership of Krystine Yaworsky and William Holmes to enhance our understanding of effective values education and provide evaluative feedback to improve future activities. Empirical evaluation and research has been central to the process since the beginning. The evaluational component is designed to help those planning a Summer Institute develop an agenda of specific issues, goals, and means to achieve these goals; to determine the effectiveness of the Institute; and to determine which features ought to be retained in future Institutes. As the process evolves, we will need to create new evaluation techniques to measure new aspects that we come to see as important.

Related to the evolution of the process at Le Moyne is the question of the program's continuity: how do you sustain such a program, insure that it continues to thrive and prosper despite inevitable changes in personnel, faculty leadership, etc.? Should we set up an independent center for the study of values education? Should our grass-roots organization be subsumed under one of the college's administrative offices? Is there some other means of insuring the program's continuity?

The matter of dissemination to other schools raises an entirely new set of questions. Beyond four-year colleges and universities, what other types of institutions—professional schools, community colleges, secondary, middle and even elementary schools—might profit from the adaptation of a program such as ours? What materials are necessary for effective dissemination to those schools? In the end, each school is going to have to ask itself a unique set of questions relating to possible implementation.

We do, however, believe that our new paradigm for education can be transplanted to a wide variety of educational institutions. Programs in other universities and colleges have tried to introduce the consideration of values into the college community. Our project is different in that we contend that it is the task of all faculty and all members of the community—not just those in campus ministry, or the philosophy or theology department—to address these issues. Our successful experience with values education prompts the Values Group to believe that we are well situated to help other institutions of higher education develop similar programs. In thinking about the best way to extend the Values Program to other institutions, we have attempted to develop a self-contained set of activities worth undertaking in its own right. But how do we motivate other institutions to consider whether or not they should use this process? We feel that once they have begun, they too will recognize the benefits we uncovered. Le Moyne is already able to point to practices that support its claim to providing a distinctive education.

In this book, we have frequently asserted that the Values Program is a process. An institution's faculty or administration will not experience the process by reading this book or thinking about its ideas. For this reason, we believe that the best way to stimulate other colleges and universities to develop values education programs is for representatives of these institutions to come to Le Moyne, experience our program, and talk with members of the Le Moyne faculty about developing similar programs at their institutions. To this end, we will invite representatives from other colleges to participate in our 1991 Summer Institute. Those visitors will need at least one year after their visit to share with their colleagues what they have experienced and to marshal the necessary interest and support to develop their own values education program. It is precisely at this point, one year after visiting Le Moyne, that the need for useful research and evaluation instruments will be most acute. At that time, the fall of 1992, the Le Moyne research effort will have produced these instruments, which will be ready for use at other institutions. We hope that ultimately this cooperation will produce valuable comparative data which will allow insight into the influence of the institutional context (e.g., college mission, composition and backgrounds of the student body, faculty characteristics, curriculum) on the effectiveness of values education efforts.

It took courage in 1984 for a small grass-roots group within the college to undertake a values audit addressing the gap between what the institution asserted in words and what it manifested through action. It also took courage in 1985 for the original seven members of the founding values group to search for a remedy to the perceived problems in the institution. This is why the Values Program is itself a model of moral courage: we are modeling both as mentors and as an institution what we are asking the students to do. No teacher can credibly encourage a student to action unless the teacher is courageous. The same truth applies to an institution. Perhaps this process has effected strategic and significant institutional change at Le Moyne College because it enables the institution to function as a role model. The power of example is that it appeals to the noblest aspirations of the human heart. In our time, when there are so few heroes left, perhaps our institutions can become heroes.

The purpose of the Values Program is quite simple: to empower students to become agents for the improvement of local, national, and global communities. We are not yet able to claim that we have accomplished this mission at Le Moyne—but we are working hard toward its fulfillment.

Endnotes

1. See Robert Jackall, *Moral Mazes: The World of Corporate Managers*, (New York: Oxford University Press, 1988).

Appendix III

1988
Summer Institute on Economic Justice

Participants:

Dr. William Bosch, S.J. . . . . .Department of History
Dr. Barron Boyd . . . . . . .Department of Political Science
Dr. Mary Collins . . . . Department of Education
Dr. Darius Conger . . . . .Department of Economics
Dr. Robert Flower . . . . Department of Philosophy
Dr. John Freie . . . . .Department of Political Science
Dr. Walter Hubner . . . . Department of Industrial Relations
Dr. Mark Karper . . . . . Department of Industrial Relations
Dr. Robert Kelly . . . . Department of Sociology
Dr. Donald Kirby, S.J. . . . . Department of Religious Studies
Dr. David Lloyd . . . . .Department of English
Dr. Roger Lund . . . . .Department of English
Dr. William Miller . . . . . . .Department of Mathematics
Dr. Dennis O'Connor . . . Department of Business Administration
Dr. David Rogers . . . . .Department of Economics
Dr. Bruce Shefrin . . . . . .Department of Political Science
Dr. Andrew Szebenyi . . . . .Department of Biology
Dr. Ronald Taylor . . . . Department of Accounting
Dr. Susan Rogers Thornton . . . . .Department of English

Facilitators:

Dr. Richard Morrill . . . . . . Past President, Centre College
Current President, University of Richmond
Dr. Kenneth Dolbeare . . . . . Professor of Political Science,
Evergreen State College
Dr. John Langan, S.J. . . . . Rose Kennedy
Professor of Christian Ethics,
Georgetown University

Coordinator:

Dr. Thomas V. Curley . . . . Professor of Philosophy
Le Moyne College

1989
Summer Institute on Peace and War

Participants:

Dr. William Barnett . . . . . Department of Religious Studies
Professor Edwin Baumgartner . . . Department of Mathematics
Dr. Susan Behuniak-Long . . . . Department of Political Science
Dr. Barbara Blaszak . . . . Associate Academic Dean
Dr. Jeffrey Chin . . . . Department of Sociology
Dr. Robert Flower . . . . Department of Philosophy
Dr. Martha Grabowski . . Department of Business Administration
Dr. Patrick Keane . . . . Department of English
Dr. George Kulick . . . . Department of Business Administration
Dr. Jill Little . . . . Department of Education
Professor William Morris . . . . . . Department of English
Dr. Nancy Ring . . . . . Department of Religious Studies
Rev. Andrew Szebenyi, S.J. . . . . . Department of Biology
Rev. Donald Zewe, S.J. . . . . . . Department of Sociology

Facilitators:

Dr. Barron Boyd . . . . Professor of Political Science
Le Moyne College
Most Rev. Thomas Costello . . . . Auxiliary Bishop
Diocese of Syracuse
Dr. David O'Brien . . . . Department of History
Holy Cross College
Dr. Roger Shinn . . . . Professor Emeritus
Union Theological Seminary

Coordinator:

Dr. Mary Ann Donnelly . . . Professor of Business Administration
Le Moyne College

1990
Summer Institute on Families and Public Policy
Participants:

Dr. Lynn S. Arnault . . . . Department of Philosophy
Dr. Harjit Arora . . . . .Department of Economics
Rev. Richard Blake, S.J. . . . . . .Department of English
Dr. Janet Bogden . . . . Department of Sociology
Dr. Sul-Young Choi . . . . Department of Mathematics
Dr. Alan Fischler . . . . .Department of English
Dr. William Foote . . . . Department of Business Administration
Dr. K. R. Hanley . . . . Department of Philosophy
Dr. Mary MacDonald . . . . Department of Religious Studies
Dr. William Shaw . . . . .Department of English
Ms. Daphne Stephens . . . . . Office of Continuous Learning
Dr. Jean Wandel . . . . Department of Education
Dr. Shawn Ward . . . . Department of Psychology

Facilitators:

Dr. Robert Kelly . . . . Professor of Sociology
Le Moyne College
Dr. Agnes Mansour . . . . Executive Director
Poverty Social Reform Institute
Farmington Hills, Michigan
Dr. Robyn Muncy . . . . .Professor of History
Le Moyne College

Coordinator:

John Langdon . . . . .Professor of History
Le Moyne College

Contributors

William R. Barnett, Ph.D.,
The Struggle for Institutional Support

Dr. William R. Barnett has been a professor of Religious Studies for 21 years—the last 13 at Le Moyne College. After receiving the Ph.D. degree from the University of Chicago, he has published research in 19th-century German and American Christian thought and has been a member of the American Academy of Religion and the American Society of Church History. He is currently completing a monograph on economic rights and religious social thought in America at the turn of the 20th century. He has become increasingly concerned with values education during the last decade. In 1990, he was appointed to the position of dean of studies at Le Moyne College.

Thomas V. Curley, Ph.D., *The 1988 Summer Institute*

Professor Curley graduated with honors from Fordham College in 1958. He received a master's degree in Philosophy in 1960, and a Ph.D. in Philosophy in 1968 from Fordham University. He is currently associate professor and chair of the Philosophy Department at Le Moyne College. He served as director of the Values Program. He is a member of the American Philosophical Association and a certified teacher-trainer for the Institute for the Advancement of Philosophy for Children.

Paul H. de Vries, Ph.D., *The Essential "Inc-Factor"*

Paul H. de Vries is the first to hold the endowed Chair in Ethics and the Marketplace at the King's College, Briarcliff Manor, New York. He completed his M.A. and Ph.D. at the University of Virginia, where his dissertation dealt with some epistemological problems in applied ethics. He has held teaching positions at five colleges and universities, including ten years at Wheaton College, Illinois, 1979-1989. At Wheaton College he was also the coordinator of General Education for three years and the founder and first Director of the Center for Applied Christian Ethics for three years. He has several published articles in the areas of applied ethics and epistemology.

Mary Ann Donnelly, Ph.D., *The 1989 Summer Institute*

Mary Ann Donnelly, professor of Business Administration, is a graduate of Le Moyne College and the Harvard Law School. A member of the New York Bar, she is active in community and college affairs and served as president of Legal Services of Central New York, chair of a Regional Pastoral Council for the Diocese of Syracuse, and president of the Le Moyne Faculty Senate. She is the co-author of a business law text, two books on bankruptcy law, and *Commercial Law* in Syracuse Law Review's Annual Survey of New York Law since 1973. Le Moyne College recognized her contributions in 1988 by naming her both "Teacher of the Year" and "Alumnae of the Year."

William Howard Holmes, Ph.D., *Power and Promise: Evaluation of an Evolving Model,* (co-author)

William Howard Holmes earned the Ph.D. degree in social psychology at the University of Massachusetts-Amherst. He is an associate professor of Psychology at Le Moyne College and an adjunct professor of Medical Humanities at the State University of New York Health Science Center in Syracuse. His teaching and research interests include attitude change and the physician-patient relationship.

Robert F. Kelly, Ph.D., *A Sociologist's Perspective*

Robert F. Kelly (Ph.D., Rutgers) is professor of Sociology at Le Moyne College and Visiting Scholar (1990-91) at the Stanford University School of Law. Kelly has conducted research and written widely on children, family law, welfare and public policy. He serves as an associate editor of the *Journal of Family Issues* and the *Journal of Marriage and the Family*. Formerly associate professor of Sociology at Wayne State University, Kelly has also held visiting appointments at Syracuse University and the University of Rochester.

Donald J. Kirby, S.J., Ph.D., *Ambitious Dreams* and *From Vision to Action.*

Donald J. Kirby, associate professor of Religious Studies, has served at Le Moyne since 1976. He is the founding and current director of the Values Program. He completed doctoral studies at Union Theological

Seminary in New York City and studied at Woodstock College in Maryland and New York, the Maxwell School of Citizenship and Public Affairs at Syracuse University, and at Le Moyne College. His teaching and research are in the areas of religion, ethics, and values with special interest in the ethical aspects of corporate policy. He has published in journals such as *Change, Liberal Education* and the *Journal of Business Ethics.* He coordinated the "Values Audit" at Le Moyne in 1984-85. He is ordained and a member of the Society of Jesus.

John W. Langdon, Ph.D., *Preface*

John W. Langdon, professor of History at Le Moyne College, earned a Ph.D. in modern European History from Syracuse University's Maxwell School of Citizenship and Public Affairs. He has taught at Le Moyne since 1971, and is a former director of the college's Honors Program and its "Teacher of the Year" in 1989. He is the author of numerous articles on French educational and European diplomatic history, and the book, *July 1914: The Long Debate, 1918-1990.*

David C. McCallum, Jr., *Two Student Perspectives* (Part 1)

A 1990 graduate of Le Moyne College with a B.A. in English and Integral Honors, McCallum has been involved in many student government and programming boards, as well as student Life as a resident advisor. He hopes to eventually be involved in higher education as a member of the Society of Jesus.

William V. Miller, Ph.D., *A Mathematician's Perspective*

An associate professor of Mathematics, William Miller has been at Le Moyne since 1982. He holds a bachelor of science degree from M.I.T. and a doctorate from the University of Michigan, both in mathematics. During 1980-81, he was a Peace Corp volunteer in Fiji, a period during which his appreciation of and sensitivity to diversity increased dramatically. For many of his current insights about education and learning, he is indebted to his 5-year-old son and 7-year-old daughter.

Alison E. Molea, *Two Student Perspectives* (Part 2)

Alison E. Molea (Le Moyne Class of 1991) is an active member in Le Moyne's International House, an organization of students who provide service to the surrounding community, nationally and internationally. She has participated in Fordham University's Global Outreach

Program, traveling to Mexico and New Mexico for the past two summers and doing van projects in needy areas. Molea is a member of Le Moyne's Integral Honors Program and pursues her deep interests in literature and writing by holding two editor positions on both Le Moyne's literary magazines. She is also a member of Le Moyne's women's lacrosse team.

Parker J. Palmer, Ph.D., *Foreword*

Parker J. Palmer completed doctoral studies in Sociology from UC-Berkeley and has taught at Beloit, Georgetown University, the Pacific School of Religion, and the Quaker Center, Pendle Hill. His work focuses on education, community, spirituality, and non-violent social change. He travels widely giving workshops, lectures, and retreats, and has often been cited as a "master teacher." One of his books on education, *To Know As We Are Known* (Harper & Row), is well known among educators in both secular and religious settings. His latest book, is *The Active Life: A Spirituality of Work, Creativity, and Caring* (Harper & Row, 1990). (His work as a "traveling teacher" was the subject of a feature article in *The Chronicle of Higher Education*, 3/28/90)

Bruce M. Shefrin, Ph.D., *The Academic Forum.*

Bruce M. Shefrin, associate professor of Political Science, was director of the first Academic Forum, 1988-89. His area of specialization is U.S. Public Policy. Publications include *The Future of U.S. Politics in an Age of Economic Limits* (Westview, 1980). Professor Shefrin will be director of the Program's fourth Summer Institute (1991) on science, technology and values.

Krystine Batcho Yaworsky, Ph.D., *Power and Promise: Evaluation of an Evolving Model,* (co-author)

Krystine Yaworsky has taught at Le Moyne College since earning a Ph.D. in Psychology at The Ohio State University in 1977. Currently she is an associate professor and chair of the Psychology Department. Her research interests include a range of topics within the field of cognitive and affective processes. Her research has addressed both theoretical and applied concerns in the areas of psychoeducational assessment, human-computer integration, and moral decision making.